Organizational Innovation

Lessons From Silicon Valley for Modernizing How Organizations Work

'Organizational Innovation' and 'OI' are both trademarks with an open license for use by people registered to coach OI, and organizations where they are working.

Learn to Coach OI at
CoachOI.com

Organizational Innovation

Lessons From Silicon Valley for Modernizing How Organizations Work

Paul C. Wilson,

Palo Alto, 'Silicon Valley'
Avebury, United Kingdom
Cape Town, South Africa
Bali, Indonesia

Copyright © 2020 Paul C. Wilson
All rights reserved.

ISBN: 9781652568186

DEDICATION

RIP Clay Christensen, who inspired me to write this book and develop a radically simple solution for the innovator's dilemma.

To the Coach OI Global Leadership team who are helping to make this happen.

Contents

How This Book Could Be Good For You	1
What to Expect	9
Transcendence in Human Consciousness	13
Silicon Valley Doesn't Want Ideas	19
Money IS Everything	31
You Can Change The World	37
Strategizing	47
Financial Feasibility	55
The Investor's Perspective	63
DESIGN	67
TRANSFORM	77
SCALE	81
Making 'IT' Happen	87
Silicon Valley Mentors	91
Silicon Valley Heroes	103
Silicon Valley Investors	113
Your Success Journey	119
Coaching OI	131
A Silicon Valley Mindset	143
Aesop Had the Right Idea	149
The Purpose of Coaching OI	151
The OI Practice Lead	169
The Role of Leadership in Innovation	179
Soul Energy	185
The Role of Managers	191
OI And Corporate Culture	199
OI and Corporate Governance	203

The OI Schedule	205
OI Principles	209
Principle 1: Coach OI	215
Principle 2: Success Journeys	219
Principle 3: DESIGN	229
Principle 4: TRANSFORM	233
Principle 5: SCALE	235
The OI Desired State	253
OI Policies and Charters	257
Building OI Capabilities	263
Implementing OI With The OI Value Chain	271
OI TRANSFORMATION	277
OI SCALE	289
OI Active!	305
Your Own OI Practice	307
The Coach OI Global Leadership Team	311
Coaching OI as a Startup	313
Coaching OI As A Service	315
About the Author	317

Part One

Introduction

1

HOW THIS BOOK COULD BE GOOD FOR YOU

What work do you do now? How many years do you expect to remain economically useful? Will you be doing the same thing for the remainder of your working life? Probably not.

>>> *If you relate to this, then, this book is for you.*

If you relate to this, then you can probably appreciate that the organization you currently work for, will probably not exist in its current form, in 20 years time. It is also unlikely that you will remain economically useful with your current skillset, for much longer.

The reason the life-span of organizations is rapidly decreasing is because they are managed by good managers who do their best to avoid organizational disruption. It's because of this, Christensen maintains, that they run great businesses into the ground. It might seem that the very same managers are going to run their employees into the ground too, for lack of adequate people development, helping employees keep up with the times. If you're one of these managers, get them a copy of this book from Amazon, and encourage them to be OI Innovators in the workplace asap!

In Christensen's book, 'The Innovator's Dilemma', one of his points is that organizations who try their hand at disruptive innovation fail because they do it with 'old thinking'. He maintains, that the organization is not flexible in terms of values about resource allocation and processes required to incubate and accelerate disruptive innovations.

His advice is that new organizations need to be created that will own the disruptive innovation and be free of the shackles of how the parent organization 'always did things'.

Whilst I agree with his point, I offer different advice. My view is that we try and innovate, hoping to provide better products or services to our customers, but when management look within for innovation that enhances the organization, they use approaches that were developed for other things. Project Management is an example, it was used to build skyscrapers, AND for a long time, to transform businesses. True, in some processes maybe the organization runs brilliantly, but why should it be in just some places? I don't think any business can say, with their hand on their heart, that everything works brilliantly. Shouldn't that be the goal? What if that was the goal of every employee? To make the cross-functional value-chain work brilliantly, and with that, every department work brilliantly? Should we even have departments?

My advice is that Organizational Innovation (OI), which has been developed specifically and only as an inward-looking innovation approach, can transform organizations into highly innovative market disruptors. I believe every employee could be doing more OI within their teams, which may well, result in more innovative customer products and services, because there'd be an internal culture of innovation, of empathy, on the whole, with an internal willingness and momentum towards positive disruption - making vast improvements.

At least, this is the lesson I learned from my experience in Silicon Valley, and I believe this is something that can be shared and developed within all organizations regardless of location. The organizations in Silicon Valley, icons like Google, Apple, Facebook, Tesla and so many others work very differently, and that is, I believe the real value of the Valley, learning how they do things, so we can be like them.

But why? Motivations could be for example, because they attract huge talent, make incredible advances in all fields and make bundles of money for their employees and shareholders whilst creating products and services that the world uses.

OI is about having employees see themselves as innovators, as a Steve Jobs, Elon Musk, or Larry Page, no matter what their job is. An Accounts Payable clerk can certainly improve the process, if only they had a collaborative, multi-faceted team to listen to them, somebody who could coach them in OI, and a corporate OI policy to encourage and support them.

In today's modern suite of enterprise software, it is a lot easier to develop solutions that are both integrated AND can be rapidly developed. Technology is not the only scope for OI.

>>> ***Any aspect of an organization can be enhanced with OI.***

Automation of blue-collar jobs has evolved now to automation of white collar jobs. Right now, the greatest breadwinner challenge in first world countries, is to remain economically useful. The chance that what you currently do is going to be done a lot cheaper, better and quicker by Artificial Intelligence in the next 15 years is substantial. Your current job will be mostly automated, that is almost guaranteed. I'd urge readers to really try to understand what this book is conveying and to implement the concepts from Silicon Valley into business and life, to create a value network around you, in your organization and community, that works in the same way, continuously innovating. Fortunately, these lessons are not difficult to understand, and it is only a matter of time before you use them naturally and become an OI Innovator, at the forefront of Organizational Innovations, within your department and/or global process in the context of a global organization.

If, for example, you're a CEO, Board Member, Marketing Director, Accounting Clerk, your job is under threat by technology that already exists. It is only a matter of when it is rolled out. It's pretty much time to drop the way you think and the methods you use to do your job and run organizations, and absolutely transcend everything you know about managing organizations. The time for disruptive Organizational Innovation is now. This has been the message of Digital Transformation for over a decade, and is often lost as 'the soft stuff' in technology departments. It's time to take tech-related OI decisions away from the IT department and give the ownership of work innovations to employees, with IT supplying capable and agile technologists who understand for example, design-thinking, and even better, the OI Value Chain. After all, how can IT know what everybody does? One of the greatest books about the future, Homo Deus (Harari), presents evidence of future, rapid advances in business process automation putting mostly all office-workers out of jobs. I think the only way to keep a salary coming in, is for employees to focus on creating the future of their department and process, always looking for ways to innovate internally.

I believe that learning how to design, transform and scale is the only personal economic future.

>>> *Everything else will be automated.*

To design, transform, and scale, is what an OI Innovator, does. Teaching others how to do OI, is Coaching OI.

This book offers a way to not only meet the future head on, but to be a contributor to the future of your organization, and your clients in the case of consultants. Certainly it's better to be co-creating the future, than being sidelined by it.

Understanding OI can help you with a practical approach and tools from *CoachOI.com* for transforming your organization to work brilliantly across the value-chain AND to better respond to the needs of your employees.

Get this right, and you will have a new skill that can be valuable in any department and organization. Then you might consider adding a few more skills and coach OI.

The question really is, how do you relate your job to new technologies? Have you found out for yourself that your job can be automated and that your future economic relevance is on the line? If so, then this book is really, really going to help you think like a Silicon Valley innovator, and find innovations that will help your team work smarter, *and* keep you relevant in your field, whilst coaching OI.

2

WHAT TO EXPECT

I worked in Silicon Valley as a founder and CEO of 4 Software startups (2 failed, 1 succeeded and 1 is still running). This book is partly my introduction story living in the valley, part research, part experiential learning. It is NOT an academic account of researched literature.

What is on offer, is a proven business approach based on Silicon Valley success stories. I call it:

>>> **Organizational Innovation**™ (OI)

OI Can be used in business, startups, government, or non-profits. It is essentially a bridge to connect what is familiar with what is new. It integrates in a single framework the DESIGN, TRANSFORM and SCALE steps, which together achieve positive internal disruptions, increasing the probability of this bridge to the new, being one that is actually useful to the employees that need it. Of course building a bridge between two places where nobody travels would be pretty useless, yet so often we make changes in business and have to use 'Change Management' to try and make employees less resistant, meaning they never wanted it in the first place.

>>>*Maybe it's time for a different way?*

In Silicon Valley I developed a concept called Success Journeys and it is essentially a focus on identifying the employee's journey (not the same as a hero or user journey) and what success means for them and what bridges they need to cross on their Success Journey. These bridges, when built in the right places, so to speak, can provide an important part of their Success Journey and if successful, the Success Journeys of many others. In OI, we speak about the 'Success Journey of the Employee'. Also, the 'Success Journey of the Team'. Many startups and business projects fail because people don't understand the principles of the Success Journey, and instead, 'mis-apply' principles that are well known, all over the world. Maybe we can look to Silicon Valley to change the way we manage internal innovations, and start focusing on transformations driven by employee-led innovation, and not just what everybody else is doing.

A Success Journey relates to both a state of consciousness, and a thought process in delivering innovations to the people that need them. Critically, is how to take the lessons from Silicon Valley and incorporate them into organizations around the world and this is the mission of a global network of OI Coaches using *CoachOI.com* as their platform to do this.

3

TRANSCENDENCE IN HUMAN CONSCIOUSNESS

Scaleable Narrow Artificial intelligence (AI) is the new(ish) kid on the block, it's smart, cheap, and reliable. Obviously it's a preferred alternative compared to humans in fulfilling specific functions, and soon, entire job roles. What sets humans apart, for now at least and the brief foreseeable future, is that we have connected human consciousness.

A way to think about consciousness is how we choose to be experienced in life, by others. It would be logical for AI to be developed to fulfill only its function. If it is a call center AI, then that's its intention. It acts on the basis of fulfilling its Call Center function. It will not give to charity, help a challenged person cross the road or create revolutions against all that is wrong with the world. AI Is like an animal, it eats, drinks and does its job, much like a trained security dog. I fully appreciate that a dog is a sentient being and is capable of building relationships with humans. So can AI. Yet, we are the master of the dog because of our superior consciousness. We have to maintain superior consciousness over AI. As long as we maintain a level of consciousness that is self-serving, acting out of fear and greed, two programmable intentions, AI will become our masters. Our low-level consciousness predictability will be leveraged by AI developers and all will be lost.

The only way forward for us mere mortals, is to leverage on our value differential in comparison to AI. I Believe that value differentiator is, *human* consciousness. In the same light, Success Journey's is a way to coach OI that involves deeply understanding employee needs, but it won't work unless ego is taken out of the coaching engagement, and the person being coached in OI, understands it's important to do the same, when assisting the Success Journeys of others, for whom they be innovating. If both can transcend their ego, their self-serving intentions and operate from a level of consciousness that creates an environment for a certain relational chemistry where trust and powerful relationships are built, then they can truly coach, and do OI. This is a key ingredient in establishing an understanding of the context of employee needs, with deep empathy, far more powerfully than simply assessment of needs. Empathy eats needs analysis for breakfast and develops intuition, the building block for higher consciousness.

Perhaps in reading this book, keep this in mind:

>>> ***Only when we listen with empathy, do we understand, and only when we live with a higher consciousness, will people ask for guidance, then and only then can we be OI Coaches.***

Everyone we meet is an opportunity to evolve our levels of consciousness, from fear and greed, to servitude of a greater humanity. So if, for you, true happiness comes from helping others, then OI as a life philosophy, can really help your Success Journey. OI As an approach aims to most importantly, help others succeed. A result of using OI to support others can really help us to be happy and more successful, financially and otherwise.

Let's look at how it's done.

Part Two

Success Journeys and The OI Value Chain

4

SILICON VALLEY DOESN'T WANT IDEAS

The number one reason for failure of most startups in Silicon Valley, is that there is no *need* for their idea. Silicon Valley wants provable *need*, using data, and makes money out of supporting specific solutions mapped to specific needs. I didn't know this at first, so let me share how I learned this in Silicon Valley.

Starting with Steve Jobs, I tried to get a sense of his journey to success.

Steve Jobs Visits Childhood Home - Photo: CNN

He always used data to develop products based on what customers wanted, not the ideas and technology the engineers developed. Search on YouTube using the term "Steve Jobs Responds to Insults." and hear this yourself.

My experiential component of understanding how Silicon Valley works, was a great experience for me, and started out something like this:

On a rainy day in February, 2016, I Uber'd a ride to Cupertino, to see Paul Jobs' house, where his adopted son, Steve Jobs, founded Apple Computers with Steve Wozniak.

I was approached by one of the neighbors who told me the stories of Steve Jobs as he knew him.

My Visit to Steve Job's Childhood Home - Where Apple Started

I loved the genuine character of the stranger who shared an intimate history of the kid who became a legend. I jumped back in the Uber and we whisked off to my next stop, Google, in Mountain View, another Silicon Valley icon, the brainchild of Larry Page and Brin Sergey. At Stanford University their project was called 'Back-rub' before it became Google, because it literally downloads or rubs the 'back' of websites to collect all the data about the site.

A Google Bicycle for Employees to Get Around Campus

I ambled into one of the canteens and got myself a 'Green Mountain' (kale smoothie) and walked outside to the famous volley-ball court we've all seen in articles about Google's culture. As I strolled closer to Larry's office, there was quite a commotion, police, bodyguards, security - apparently the President of Indonesia had come to meet with Larry.

Indonesian President Joko Widodo Visits Google : techinasia.com

Seriously...consider that for a moment, the president of a country with a population of 265 Million people, goes to Larry's office. This fact was startling to me.

What does Google do? Simply, it gives people a way, to help them on their personal and business success journeys. Whilst this is happening, Google shareholders are winning.

Later I went to Facebook and lunched in one of the many awesome canteens they have, thanks to a friend of mine who worked there.

One of Facebook's Canteens

I wondered philosophically, what does Facebook do? The same as Apple and Google, it gives people ways to be successful in their journeys, family, career, social, and now in business, enabling them to setup online shops on facebook... and shareholders get richer whilst Facebook does this.

Days later, after a $10 founder's haircut, I lay on the lawn of Hewlett Packard Enterprise complex on Hanover Street and I started realizing a pattern...

All of these Silicon Valley icons got to be monumentally successful because they had all followed the same steps, helping people to be successful at something. This is very different to a needs analysis. It involves strategy and empathy. We'll cover both in later chapters of this book.

For the next 2 years, I studied their workings to determine what the common steps were in their journeys to success. During this study, I developed a method of working based on the steps I discovered, and called it:

>>> **The OI Value Chain.**

For the OI Value Chain to work, we need to start with what employees need to be successful in their job and career, which is different to how we've 'always done things'. But putting the needs of others first, is a change in thinking for many and needs its own focus and approach. I call this focus:

>>> **The Success Journey of the Employee**

The Success Journey™ method is a way for OI Coaches to help employees and teams, and to help them to approach others and assist in solving real problems, not the perceived problems which has been the downfall of so many business projects.

Highly effective business improvements are all about the 'Success Journey - of The Employee'. It's about helping employees to be successful, in THEIR Success Journey and starts with data about employee's needs. To help implement the Success Journey approach, which produces large amounts of data, I built an OI Platform to serve as an integrated cloud database for OI Value Chain workflows, business-case modeling, data-capturing, essentially it's an OI 'System of Records'.

Ironically, it seems to be a fact that if your focus is other people's success, you will succeed yourself. However, and with this disclaimer, let that be a by-product, not your intention or purpose. I mean, don't help others, with the intention of helping yourself, if you want to be sustainably successful. It seems counter-intuitive, but the world shows this to be the truth. Steve Jobs passed away with a fortune to his name, Priscilla and Mark Zuckerberg committed to giving away most of their money.

For those who have succeeded, the focus has never been money, unless at times, it was in seriously short supply! It's been about building stuff for other's needs, to achieve success. When Apple surpassed Microsoft in market value, Steve Jobs responded in an interview that it was never a motivator at Apple, to be more valuable than Microsoft, because it didn't add any value, in giving customers great products.

I believe now, after researching Silicon Valley heroes, that if you are a natural innovator (7-15% of people), just like them, your natural purpose is to help others on their Success Journeys - so the start of any Success Journey requires being human, being present to the needs of others, and that requires empathy.

The research and analytics I've gathered indicate that the market does not care what *you as an organization,* want, what you can do, what you're selling. The market only cares about how you are going to help them on their Success Journey. Trust me...other people are important in fulfilling your own Success Journey, but you HAVE TO make it about their needs, where you can help them, not the great idea you have, or great new app you built. IT Departments around the world have worked opposite to how Silicon Valley works, since the beginning of their reign on technical innovations in organizations, pushing their tech to users. They got away with it because they had a 'captive market', employees had to use what they pushed out. If they showed resistance, they would tell the business to do 'Change Management' as if it was the silver bullet, which if business got wrong, then business would be held responsible for employees not using the tech that IT pushed. I'm certain that IT departments never had any fun doing this, I'm also pretty sure they want to work differently and make apps that their colleagues *WANT* to use. The good news, is that there is a better way. "Lead with the need" is a well-known sales quote, and it applies to OI too. In fact it's a key principle in OI, why shouldn't we lead with the employee's need when it comes to trying to make the organization work better? Shouldn't we be looking at what the employee needs to do better in their job? Think bigger too, what do they need to succeed in their career? And...what if this works so brilliantly, it can be sold to other organizations? So really 'The Success Journey of The Employee' comes into focus, in OI, for many reasons. We really want to understand what they think they 'need to succeed', I found that in Silicon Valley, organizations are very responsive to the work needs of the employee. The flashy work environments, the great canteens etc. aren't just for show, it's evidence of a deeper culture of listening to the employee's needs and creating a total environment that responds to what employees need, to do great work. OI Must lead with the 'needs to succeed' of the employee, otherwise OI will fail and organizations will never be as successful as the ones in Silicon Valley, and may continue their slow decline into obscurity.

Here's proof about needs being important, in data:

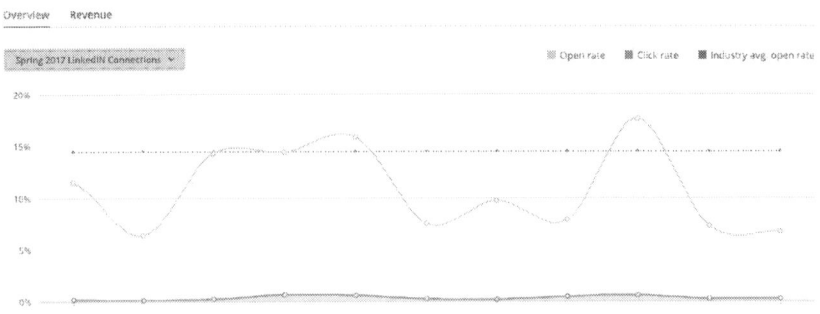

Graph Showing Email 'Open & Click' Statistics Introducing People to Our App

The graph shows 11 email campaigns over 3 months with different subject lines and content, sent to 14,000 people, (before GDPR). The 'large-wave' line indicates the number of email opens per campaign. When the subject line included something that related to their needs, it crossed the industry average, indicated by the straight line (just under 15%). The 'small-wave' line at the bottom indicates the number of clicks on a link to our OI Platform. This went from .3% to 1.4% when the app was introduced as something that solves people's OI and transformation problems. That's a 4.6 times improvement in interest to read an email.

Everything below the industry standard line (14%), was an email campaign about features the app had and how great it worked. Very few people clicked to read it. Proving that generally, nobody cares about you or what you're selling.

They only care about what can help them with their particular problem and they need clear messaging on how that's going to happen, efficiently curated by somebody they trust. For many this will be obvious, but for 'left-brained' people like myself, it's a very difficult thing to shift from so-called 'left-brain' to 'right-brain' thinking. This data provides an evidence-based person, the evidence to be more empathic to people, when doin OI. Pushing apps to employees happens a lot in IT Projects for example, where users are sent emails about the new system being implemented and doesn't consider for a moment how some employee pains are going to be removed, or where they might benefit from the new system in their job.

This data indicates clearly, you will not succeed in Silicon Valley, as long as you're trying to tell people what it is that you're doing and what your product or service does. Do the research on what they need, or may need in the future and build your product on this data. Communicate it in a similar way, which becomes your market message and has to resemble the needs phraseology of your market. We call this the market/message fit. After two years of not earning a salary, and determinedly focussed on learning how the valley works and how to be successful with a great product, suddenly, only recently do the words of the Silicon Valley heroes make sense to me, beyond just the inspiration of their virtual and real-life presence. They all say, find the pain point, fit a product, fit the message and scale. Or simply...

>>> *Nail it and scale it!*

So, the first principle, as a context for the following chapters, is that people don't care about you, but to do great Organizational Innovations, you have to care about people. You have to ask, what do they need on their Success Journey? So to coach OI well, it's something we should already be passionate about, because that's what people need from us, it's what employees who want to innovate, need from us. The Success Journey - of The Employee helps to start that process.

5

MONEY IS EVERYTHING

My $1,800 a Month Bunk-Bed, in Mountain View

You don't have to come to Silicon Valley to learn how it works, that's the purpose of this book. To save you paying $1800 a month for a bunk-bed, in a hacker-hostel, shared with five other people of extremely annoying sleeping habits AND 2 showers with 22 people, keeping it quick and often cold.

The lessons I learned in the hacker-hostel in Mountain View (Google's hometown), were useful, for one reason and one reason only. I learned that there is a war for innovation, and in that war, money is everything. Not capital funding that is given to you, but money that you can save bootstrapping. Bill Gates says that "Success is not a good teacher", I agree.

In OI, if we can get to a working prototype of whatever the OI is, without having to get money from a budget, we're starting off on the right foot, even if it's a temporary situation just to prove it works and meets the needs of the employee and the team. This is how Silicon Valley works!

>>> The best OI will need no budget!

BTW Don't try a startup in the valley, unless you have either existing customers that can sustain you here, or a 'deep-pocket' Angel Investor. But, if you absolutely have to come here, try before March, or after August. The time between this period is Summer Intern season which drives accomodation prices sky-high.

Places to Sleep are Scarce in the Valley - left $1800 per month for a bunk bed, right, where I paid $400 a month sleeping in some guys scrappy back yard.

The essence of this message, is that budget processes are stodgy at best. If an OI can be developed, at least to prove that, budget invested in the OI, will be a good decision then it will be a lot easier. Creating an OI budget business case once the prototype has been in play, means also that there is more data to substantiate the funding of scaling up the OI in the organization, regionally or globally. Ultimately, OI success creates value for all stakeholders, where financial wealth is one aspect of the end-goal. Let's be frank, money is a scarce resource almost everybody is in need of more money, (except maybe 10,000 people in the whole world). If average people were to calculate how much money would be needed to carry them and their loved ones through the next 50, 60 ,70 years of their life, it's a lot!

So we have to be realistic, money is a motivator for the individual OI Innovator, why shouldn't they be rewarded for a great OI? Let's consider finances to be really, really important in employee's Success Journey and find ways to reward the employee who went through the OI Value Chain and created wealth for the organization. Go ahead, frame that OI feasibility in millions from savings and or revenue, but there is a way to calibrate that top-down view with a bottom-up view, we'll show you how in a later chapter.

Halloween at Steve Jobs' house in Professorville, Palo Alto

Back in the Mountain View hacker-hostel, I spent a lot of time talking to the hostess who I came to appreciate and regard highly. She shared with me her stories about the valley. What became evident, is that the stories behind the stories you read, are so much more interesting and intellectually stimulating. I learned where the Silicon Valley heroes liked to hang out, I learned about Singularity University (Peter Diamandis), I learned about Steve Jobs' habits, where he used to walk. I also found, quite by accident, Tesla's head office in the rolling hills of Stanford University's 'farm'. I was in love with the Valley, but for all the wrong, material reasons that drive flocks of startup founders here, to experience what I was experiencing. San Francisco, the northern most point of Silicon Valley, has always attracted people wanting their piece of the Gold Rush. The high excitement is economically beneficial for the area.

My motivation was to become a Silicon Valley hero, to push my app onto the world, and like everybody else, who tried it the wrong way around, I failed. Although I was a generation older than the valley's genius computer scientists, my journey was inspired partially from their eagerness and passion to get rich and change the world. This inspiration lighted the desire to pay $1800 a month for a bunk-bed, a desire to ignore everything else and to work freakishly hard on my product, which like everybody else's, also failed (2016 was the worst year for startups in recent Silicon Valley history, no excuse, my product predictably sucked anyway).

This WAS the start of my Success Journey, I realized this a year later. Fail often, fail hard, and I did. But *I* was so focussed on what *I* wanted to push into the world, what *I* needed, and *I* was blinded by the FINANCIAL successes of the icons around me. Success is a poor teacher, and maybe narcism is the ultimate weakness.

But after being there, in the trenches of Silicon Valley, life has improved. The lessons have finally been learned, what the Silicon Valley heroes have been trying to tell us - and I can now share with you, and you can share in your organization.

6

YOU CAN CHANGE THE WORLD

The previous chapter was about giving you a sense of the purpose of 'Success Journeys of The Employee', as a business strategy and a brief feeling for what it's like in Silicon Valley. This chapter is the beginning of the Success Journey approach to helping employees succeed. When approaching employees who are potential OI Innovators, when we coach OI, the messaging is crucial. Steve Jobs was a genius at messaging, which means, communicating about something. He made you feel like Earhart, Ghandi, Edison, Callas, etc. He truly believed that for example, Einstein would have used a Mac, and *implied in that message* is: "If you're smart, you'd use a Mac too."

 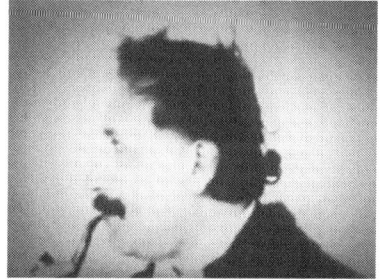

He really made you feel that Apple was going to save you from Orwell's '1984', so you can be free to do what YOU want and break molds. Message is everything and must match the other's aspirations, with the OI Messaging too. He knew that a percentage of the world's population were all about 'Thinking different and changing the world.'. So he positioned market messages to appeal to anybody on that journey, implying that having a Mac, was part of the journey.

When we coach OI, our messaging to employees who are potential OI Innovators, is that they have the potential to Change the World, within the organization, who will in turn, support the employee through the OI Value Chain and reward suitably, so long as the messaging in the OI Feasibility is spot on. 7-15% Of employees will respond to that message. Next is to position OI Coaches as being an important part of that journey.

I genuinely believe Steve expected Apple users to make the world a better place, because as he put it "It's kind of messed up in a lot of ways, but you can change it, you can mold it...".

Steve Jobs Philosophy on Life Interview

The point of this chapter, and the start of any Success Journey, is the discussion about the employee, the potential OI Innovator. This is the person you want to get, reaching out to you, when they want to be coached in OI. Why? Because the person you are going to assist through the OI Value Chain, is the person who is going to create extra wealth for the organization *and* themselves. The only way to create positive emotional connection with employees, is when you are trusted and have a sincere interest in their needs, and show it in your messaging with clear consistency in all communications. Remember:

>>> ***Empathy is the beginning of the Success Journey!***

When we're coaching OI and talking to employees, we will sense this as we ask them about their Success Journeys. Go ahead and try, with sincerity, reach out to any employee and ask them "What's your Success Journey, in your job, in your career? What's your strategy for success?" Help them understand that you're genuinely eager and interested to learn more about them. You can ask them, genuinely with a deep-seated pure intention, to serve if you can, ask:

>>> *"What does success mean to you in the workplace, in your career? What's your life Success Journey look like?"*

This will open a discussion and create space which you can learn from, whilst exercising being present in your own mind, from a place of empathy. Stanford University taught me this in their design-thinking workshops (d.school).

At the Stanford University School of Design (d.school)

This space you have created with the other, talking about their Success Journey, is the foundation of your new relationship with that person.

From that moment on, you CAN BE the bedrock for their Success Journey, and you are on your way to coaching OI. This is where you can really shine in helping employees achieve success. When coaching OI, YOU no longer exist! Now, it's all about your OI Innovators, the employees who want to innovate and recognize the future needs them. My mistake in the Valley, was believing that I was so smart and that I had built something so great, investors would write me checks on the basis of a simple product informational email.

Sequoia Capital, arguably the best Venture Capital firm in the valley.

I sent hundreds of emails to the valley's Venture Capital (VC) firms and investors (thousands) and received 3 replies (All regrets, but thank you Khosla Ventures, Sequoia Capital and SVAngel).

This applies to OI too. People aren't going to let you waste money innovating, unless there's a good business case for the OI, and that means, a very clear employee need. The days of IT departments innovating in their own Ivory Tower, then pushing software out to users are over, especially with the new SAP Innovation Technologies which allow IT departments to build apps on the SAP platform, with deep integration to SAP S/4HANA.

Back to the war of innovation in Silicon Valley. Of a thousand startups, 10 may succeed to survive to the next year - what a fool I was to believe I'd be one of them.

Only because of a last minute angel investor, I persisted into year 2. In my startup adventure, I went through a pivot (product or business change of direction) amazingly complete strangers believed in what I was doing and I was emotionally and financially supported to continue, family, friends and new investors spurred me on, all thanks to them! In an organization, an OI may pivot in its design or a new problem definition may reveal a deeper seated opportunity to innovate. Pivots happen in life all the time and will happen in OI too.

After a team break-up, I closed ChangeNexus and started in a new direction, carrying over my investors and advisers.

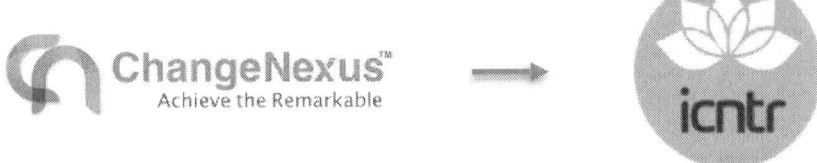

Based on my own problem of trying to get a startup running in Silicon Valley, I started an OI Platform. Basically it integrates and automates over 500 data points in the DESIGN, TRANSFORM, SCALE aspects of innovative disruption for an enterprise. I detract...here's the thing: in Silicon Valley, emotional support is great in Success Journeys but YOU are ultimately responsible for validation and traction with complete strangers known as customers and that requires grit, discipline and consistency.

As Elon Musk says, if you need motivational talks to get you doing something, *you're doing the wrong thing*!

So what I learned in the Valley, is the first principle of a Success Journey, it's that, it is NOT about you, it's NOT about your abilities, needs and wants and self-appreciation. It's all about the people with the need. How well do you understand them, their plans and pains?

Make this clear to anybody you help on their Success Journey too. For them to be successful, they have to focus on their own coworker's needs, and the needs of *their* team, in order to be successful at creating more value. This focus will become a part of the culture and spread to customers and supplier relationships too. So it's about helping employees to help their teams at an individual and team level.

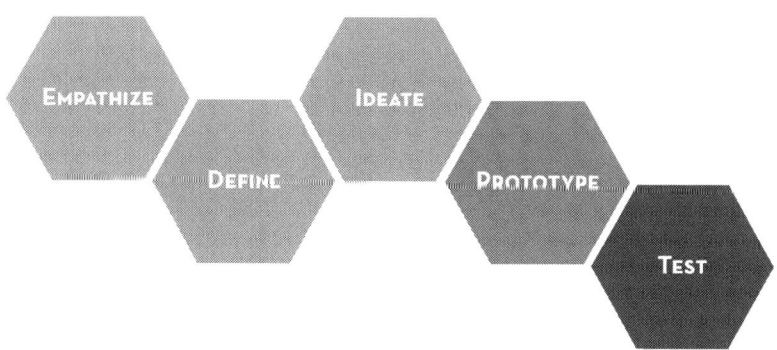

Stanford Design School - Design Thinking Process

Intellectually it makes no sense, but when you coach OI, YOU have to leave the primal brain of fear and greed, and move into empathy and focus on others. This is part of evolving your consciousness and beating AI, getting more meaning out of life, amongst other things. One of the most brilliant people I ever met, David Kelley, started Design Thinking. He is incredibly empathic, he is also head of engineering at Stanford University, so he's incredibly left-brained, and also runs the Design School, so he works with right brain too.

This is the ultimate goal in coaching OI, to be able to work with a high degree of effectiveness, on technical as well as, human aspects of the organization.

In the Valley, if you can do this first, be empathic, you will save at least a year of misdirected focus, substantial loss and maybe even give up on YOUR Success Journey. Empathy is the opposite of narcissism and probably the most important aspect of one's self to work on. Get this right and you will have created genuine purpose, you'll be benevolent and in servitude to others. If you achieve this, you're starting down the path of a Silicon Valley hero. Don't believe me? Consider this, AirBNB gave home-owners tools to earn and travelers to save money, there's clear value creation for others. Stanford University, the source of Silicon Valley's legendary beginnings at HP, gave people the education to create Success Journeys for markets and humanity. OI Coaches need to understand everything is about others and how to help them on their Success Journeys, that's your Value Proposition when coaching OI.

7

STRATEGIZING

Once your employees who have been identified as potential OI Innovators, reach out and want to be coached in OI, and have been through a discussion about their Success Journey, the first thing to co-discover with them, is the game-plan or strategies for their Success Journey to take shape. Remarkably, one of the benefits of such a discussion is a deeper relationship with the employee, *and it becomes personal*! As the other person unpacks their ideas for progressing their Success Journey, the idea of purpose (why) may begin to arise. Where the other becomes excited about a particular discussion or direction, that is where purpose comes to the forefront. It's important to unpack purpose and extract things like values, the moral compass for the journey. The character also comes out, and certain themes become evident. These are all important in setting the building blocks of the strategy or strategies. This book is not about becoming an MBA graduate, so we don't want to get into Strategy Theory here. Perhaps just a simple way to think about strategy is just a 'Vision' or 'Game Plan' for how the 'Mission' or 'Purpose' is going to be realized - the stories in this game-plan, are your strategies. Each strategy includes goals, from these goals, struggles to achieve goals are identified. These struggles come into focus as being where employees need help. It's important, when creating strategies to do a SWOT analysis, with the employee. This means looking at opportunities and threats, then determining what strengths to leverage to meet some opportunity. Conversely, what weakness need to be strengthened to prevent some threat. Here's an example:

My Purpose: "To help organizations discover OI."
My Game-Plan: "To build OI awareness."
One of my strategies is:
"To use my knowledge (strength) of how Silicon Valley organizations innovate internally, to meet a global need (opportunity) of readers wanting to learn new business skills, thereby creating awareness of OI."
One of my strategic GOALS is: "To write a book.""
This strategic goal indicates potential strategic needs, such as a proofreader, editor and publisher.

Do you know your employee's strategic goals? Does the employee know the organization's strategic goals? Or even the department or team's strategic goals?

Can you deduce what needs they may have? Do you know their goals that haven't been set yet, where you might help?

When an employee, the OI Innovator thinks of an innovative way to be more successful, related to themselves, coworkers or the team, that isn't an OI. It's just an idea.

>>> ***OI isn't about some idea you 'got'.***

But it's a start. In coaching OI, after an iterative discussion in the first coaching session, with a potential OI Innovator about what they want to do, and the reason they want to do it (avoid complicating this discussion too much), then ideas will evolve, designs will (pivot) anyway, so don't get caught up on setting anything permanent. Most of the well-known Silicon Valley brands pivoted to something else. So, very simply, help them to clarify and know what they want to do, and help them be sure on their 'why', which may also evolve as they grow in their success, or learn from failure. When coaching OI, facilitate this process with the OI Innovator. My 'Why?' is that I want to help you to coach OI, to achieve a high degree of value in your organization and *sidestep* the

President Trump Pulls Out   Prime Minister Macron Counters President Trump

coming automation of jobs. Game plans can be great when simple. Easy enough to communicate and easy enough to remember daily as the driving force behind a product, a team, a business. So everything one does on their Success Journey needs to have a reason, and that reason has one or more strategies that have been formulated for successful accomplishment of the purpose, through a vision or game-plan. For example, climate change defense is a global strategy. More was the emotional response about a collectively supported strategy being weakened by the decision of one man, than the strategy itself. More to the point, President Trump felt that his responsibility to his constituents, was to reject the strategy agreed upon by the entire world (mostly) and to propose a new one. This happens a lot in business too, when new execs arrive. How others responded will be recorded in history forever. However, the people Trump represented apparently felt like their needs were being met, in for example, Philadelphia.

Welcome to the idea of competing strategies. The reason for mentioning this point, is the importance in understanding that strategies drive innovation, they can also stop innovation. Regardless, competition will be there. There is a 'thing' that fuels strategies to have impact and that thing is 'Stakeholder Agenda'. There will be competing OIs in the same organization, the best OI will win, and that's what makes innovation so unique in delivering positive disruption. OI Coaches need to be needed by the natural innovators (7-15% of employees). There's a bell-curve, OI is NOT going to be appreciated by everybody. Innovators will love OI, early adopters will appreciate it, but late adopters and laggards won't. The Paris Climate Accord is a disruptive innovation, the iPhone was a disruptive innovation. But they don't get everybody's buy-in.

Depending on the purpose and strategies you may consider in your Coaching OI game plan for your clients or organization, be clear on if you're targeting innovators or laggards. Then establish what the majority of their needs are. Are you going to help create change, or stop it?

It's ok to go over purpose and strategy again and again in cycles. This is what many executives do all the time. Sit in ivory towers, either patting each other on the back, or tackling each other, to agree on just what the heck to do, to sustain and grow their business. As your job is to facilitate other people's Success Journeys, simply understanding what their need is, is enough to start the next step in Success Journeys. So for now, getting a specific idea of what the other needs, might be better if simple like '...organize the world's information and make it universally accessible and useful." - simple doesn't mean easy.

> "Google's mission is to organize the world's information and make it universally accessible and useful"
>
> – Google

8

FINANCIAL FEASIBILITY

Think like an investor...the OI 'Pitch' or 'Business Case' ultimately determines whether to do this thing or not. We've seen the SharkTank horror stories on TV. Much the same and in a similar routine procedure, senior managers and executives have to pitch the business case for the Capital Expenditures and Operating Expenditures (CAPEX and OPEX) they need to achieve the business goals for their division or department, for the next year, and then show variances by quarter, sometimes by month.

From the perspective of an OI Innovator, the employee who wants to do an OI, it is really difficult most of the time to clearly state how you understand the financial impacts of an OI. A large part of what the OI Innovator will continuously do, is to think, to just forget about it. Nobody likes working out the details of an organization's success and how to achieve it, unless there's a payout for them, a fat healthy payout.

Here's how it Silicon Valley does it...

Firstly, I'm going to introduce you to what dreamers and high-level thinkers do all the time, called the 'Top-Down' view (TAM), and then I'm going to introduce you to what will either be the rocket that blows up the founder's dreams, or the rocket that will launch them into the stratosphere called 'Bottom-Up' (SOM).

So first, the easy part:

Top-Down: This is normally the job of the marketing department. Top-Down approach is known in Silicon Valley as Total Addressable Market, or TAM.

TAM is the most fun working out, this is where the founder's heart will race and their eyes, shine. Here's an example of a TAM exercise, with a fictitious new product.

<u>The tickyRing</u>. So let's say you have gone through a cinema user experience with a few people and realized that there seems to be a common need with cinema customers, for a movie ticket holder. This meets a need, a pain point, that when people go to movies/cinema, they can carry their popcorn and drink without trying to balance one on their forearm whilst they reach for their movie ticket when the ticket checker asks for it : the person making sure you have a

ticket (bet you've done this right?). You design a bamboo-made ticket holder which is a cup-sized ring that fits around your drink cup and you can clip your ticket into this ticket holder, so you can hold your popcorn and drink, with your tickets clipped into your bamboo invention.

You call it the 'tickyRing'. Now people can get their popcorn and drink, slip the cup into their tickyRing and clip their movie ticket into the tickyRing so the ticket checker simply takes the ticket, whilst you hold your snacks, and replaces the stub after tearing off their piece of the ticket, back on the tickyRing, in a way that you can easily see your seat number.

Now let's calculate the TAM.

At least one report says that 1.68 Billion people go to movies annually around the world (2011). We can keep that figure the same for 2017, because although the global population is growing, online movie services like Netflix, and expensive ticket pricing means cinema attendance as a percentage of population is on the decline. To continue our TAM calculation, we price our tickyRing at $5 (it's organic, responsibly-grown bamboo). So our TAM is $8.25 Billion. In other words, if every movie goer bought your tickyRing, you'd have a market of $8.25 Billion (1.68 Billion * $5). Sounds like a great idea right?

OK, let's bring that figure down to earth.

Bottom-up calculation, or SOM, the serviceable obtainable market. But before we get to that, as Ranjeeta Singh, an IoT specialist in the Bay Area, points out, we have to identify the SAM, or Serviceable Available Market. This is, in the tickyRing example, the number of people who actually have this pain point. So perhaps we find that only 75% of people buy snacks when going to movies, which leave their hands occupied and unable to reach for their movie ticket and thus have the pain point.

Calculating the SOM means we have to work within the SAM number, or 75% of movie goers who have this pain point. SOM or Serviceable Obtainable Market, relates to the revenue opportunity within your current and planned geographic range. There are 130,000 movie cinemas around the world. How many can you get to? In Silicon Valley there are about ten cinema complexes. After researching with each, I establish that there are approximately 800,000 people who go to movies in this area.

I'm about to introduce you to a new term: Disruption Scales. So I calculate my first Scale Plan which is local cinemas. So SAM = movie goers who have this pain point (800,000 * 75% = 600,000) * $5 for the tickyRing =

$3,000,000 revenue. Congratulations that's your SOM, big difference right? $ 8,250,000,000 vs. $3,000,000, that's .05% of TAM.

Get the idea? Go ahead and plan for world domination, but do it with a bottom-up approach. You have to do this SAM and SOM calculation and be clear about how you are going to achieve that figure using Scale Plans which is how you get to your customers (more on this later).

Now to put this data into a Pitch (Business Case) you'd have to start with these figures from your TAM, SAM and SOM calculations. Then you'd have to show data, in other words, how many people, based on research you've done, have this pain point (SAM) are within your reach and would buy a tickyRing (SOM). If it's 25% of your SAM market or 600,000 * 25%, at $5 then your target market will give you $ 750,000.

You'd also have to design the tickyRing, patent it, trademark it etc. These setup and project costs need to be factored into your pitch. Key here too, is how long would you take to get that revenue. Three years maybe? How many SCALE Plans would you need? In other words how would the tickyRing team physically, through actual work activities, grow to 25% of the targeted movie goers in Silicon Valley? What would be the other Scale Plans plans for rolling out to the whole of California? America? The World? Pitching these different revenue SCALE Plans is key in showing how the founder will get to the bottom-up figures, and how they intend to grow. The same applies to the OI Feasibility study within an organization. The OI Innovator, when being coached OI, will detail how the targeted employees adapt to the OI in the organization and what the top or bottom line benefits are going to be, thereby generating, in simple terms, the OI business case and ROI for internal organization innovations, or new products and services for customers. The Business Case will help to partly answer the OI Feasibility question.

Below is the essence of the OI Pitch:

Show TAM, Show SAM, SOM, Show Investment Required - (Costs to Setup, Design, Transform, Scale)

Show Scale Plans:
Scale Plan 1 : Target Market 1 Revenue
Scale Plan 2 : Target Market 2 Revenue
Scale Plan 3 : Target Market 3 Revenue
Show Total Scale Plan Revenues

Therefore Business Case Return on Investment (ROI) is:
Savings or Profit Earnings / Investment

Of course you need to break this up into years, and months. Maybe even weeks. Then you need to divide your ROI by the number of financial periods it would take to get that balance sheet 'added-value', giving you a

        Rate of Return - ROI / Years.

See more about pitches on sites like 500 Startups. Can you translate this easily into the context of an OI? Register as a free member at *CoachOI.com* and see a few examples and how to create and manage OI Feasibility.

9

THE INVESTOR'S PERSPECTIVE

Try this, using any maps app, search for Palo Alto, then with Palo Alto in focus, search for 'venture', as in 'venture capital'. What you will see, are hundreds of dots appearing in what is actually a fairly small location. If you didn't know, Palo Alto is the 'soul' of Silicon Valley and geographically more or less the middle.

The business of Venture Capitalists is to funnel funds from registered investors or institutes into selected startups. Some of them are wealthy people, channeling their own funds (angels). Some of them are people acting as if they have money, only to see what you're working on. Some of these fake Venture Capitalists are serving the interests of foreign nations, sharing the latest greatest innovation decks in Silicon Valley, received from startup founders, with their friends back home, including the usual suspects. One of my early apps was copied in this fashion, *and* the marketing material, they hardly bothered to even change the marketing narrative, just kept it all the same, I won't shame any nations, but you might guess who. Just saying, don't trust anybody you don't know, do research on who you're sending your pitch deck to.

From the perspective of genuine investors, and this also means the organization you might work for, disruptive innovations don't have a market yet, so there's no future data upon which to make an investment decision. Christensen elaborates on this in his book 'The Innovator's Dilemma'. I surmise that there are two tricks that investors use to ascertain if there is a market or not. Firstly, invariably, VC's make decisions on fundamental technology trends. The 4th industrial revolution includes for example, drones, AI, Robotics, Internet of Things (IoT), autonomous vehicles and others. Consequently, VC's (Venture Capitalists) are investing almost only in innovations that include these disruptive technologies. Whether or not your organization will take the same investment principles in terms of what technologies to use within the organization, depends on how well OI is working in your organization, in terms of identifying internal use-cases for these technologies.

Certainly the 4th Industrial Revolution offers clarity on where organizations might consider focussing their technology OI investments. Ten years ago, mobile, social, big data and cloud were determined as the drivers of economic growth, and they were right. Data drives this research and data is all that matters when it comes to OI too.

The second trick investors use, is to only invest where there is clear data on who has what pains, known as a 'use-case'. So whilst it is impossible to determine exact amount of value an OI can create, an organization can assess where the organization has pains. This data can drive resource allocation decisions and spawn new departments even, and capabilities.

Data showing clear needs, is what gets investors in Silicon valley excited and what can get CEOs and executives in established organizations excited about. Not data about where existing organizational activities might improve, known as continuous business improvements, but rather positively-disruptive innovations promising to alleviate pains in the organization, and maybe even have a positive impact on the market.

Essentially, every organizational manager, at all levels, is a Venture Capitalist. They're either making resource allocations to keeping things as they are, or they're allocating part of their resources to building the future. Only the latter will result in sustainable returns.

To be clear, developing ideas into reality, but not focussed how it's going to meet current or future organizational needs, based on which employees currently have specific pains, is a waste, (I should know!). OIs Won't attract investment or budget in an organization, without OI Feasibility and Value Mapping analysis being done with some significant measure of confidence in that data and the potential for returns, with a set of issues, risks, and assumptions clearly articulated - the details matter! This is what is driving the massive demand for data scientists and experience data, which organizations like Qualtrics (Owned by SAP) focus on getting.

I was stupid when I started my startups. I didn't have data on who has pains that my solution would fix.

I hypothesized...when I should have been getting data about the problem!

In an 'OI Active' organization, coaches can keep data from the OIActive system, on hand or memorized, about specific OIs. This can be really helpful, checking the OI platform can become your second nature, just like checking social media. If a coach is walking around the organization's campus with clipboards, virtual or otherwise, always with OI data in hand, it makes for effective casual standup OI chats and encounters.

10

DESIGN

In only a few moments people make decisions to use something or not. After that point it becomes increasingly difficult to change their mind.

What exactly is the decision?

It's this: *Will this 'thing' help me on my Success Journey?*

Jobs and Woz Innovating - Using a Familiar Keyboard form a typewriter for their first computer.

AND The more familiar it is, the better. It's as simple as that. So whatever the OI Innovator is doing, the absolute definite purpose of that OI must be to remedy a pain or need, or something that can help other employees in their job. It can't just be one employee. (There are exceptional cases where it would ok. These 3 motivators (Pain, Gain, Help) creates an opportunity to innovate. This is the essence of needs opportunity mining. Sometimes called 'value proposition' work. If your value proposition is not clear and doesn't motivate you to get out bed in the morning with zest and focus, you haven't got it right yet. People are discouraged from trying to retro-fit a value-proposition to a product. In a famous Steve Jobs video, he responds to an engineer who was criticizing Jobs for turning down great technical products. Steve responded by saying that you don't sit down with engineers, make the tech work, then figure out a way to sell it. It's the other way around.

Facebook Founder's Family, Priscilla, Mark & Daughter, 'Max'

When I first came to Silicon Valley, my purpose was to make bundles of money and retire. What I failed to notice was that all the Silicon Valley heroes I was studying, were STILL EMPLOYED AT THEIR STARTUPS, or had been until near death. Steve Jobs' last day at Apple was only months before he passed away, here's the thing, he didn't need the money! They had made piles of money AND THEY WERE STILL WORKING.

David Kelley and I having a chat.

David Kelley founder of IDEO (Designs pretty much everything cool in the world) and Stanford Design School, said that innovation is simply taking two old ideas and making a new one. Many things have been said about innovation but here I'd offer that innovation is describing a product or service that is the successful result of a value-chain, and that the three key steps are:

>>> ***DESIGN, TRANSFORM, SCALE***

Before one can even get to the design whiteboard, the needs of the other must be recorded. Even Steve Jobs used DATA to drive what to design. He wasn't a design genius, he was a data genius. Steve's vision and courage was in making decisions about future hypothetical direction of implied technology needs of his market, but always based on data. This is also why Tim Cook, who took over from Steve Jobs as Apple's CEO, has been great in continuing the success of Apple, because they work with incredible discipline, based on Supply Chain data.

Steve Jobs Using Data to Identify Market Needs

Tim Cook Announces 1 Billion iPhones Sold

Tim is definitely one of my Silicon Valley heroes, primarily because he hasn't screwed up Apple, when it could have been so easy to do so. People think his focus should be on disruptive innovation, but I'd argue that they're wrong. His focus is on sustaining innovations, not disruptive innovations. Steve Jobs did the disruptions, Tim Cook's job is to sustain the disruptions.

Data shows that if he tried to be disruptive, he would fail - Apple does electronic devices and media content channels. That's it.

Tim's job is not to disrupt, but to continue scaling current innovations and continue sustaining the relevance of existing successes (new versions).

Elon Musk Shares Opportunities
and Insights Openly

When you're talking to an employee about their Success Journey, do a sense check of their own needs assessment, get them to fill the blanks, in the following paragraph:

EXAMPLE:

"In order to realize my purpose, and achieve my strategic goal of <u>retiring comfortably at 55</u>, and from the perspective of <u>job remuneration</u> I need to <u>rapidly start</u> OI activities in my area of the <u>efficient spend</u> Strategy more specifically <u>capital projects</u>. This will benefit <u>our capital efficiency</u>, so that the organization can achieve <u>better use of capital</u>, thereby helping them realize their needs of <u>a 0.2% margin increase, resulting in $3 million added value</u>."

Go ahead:

"In order to realize my purpose, and achieve my strategic goal of _____, and from the perspective of _____ I need to _____ OI activities in my area of _____ Strategy more specifically _____. This will benefit _____, so that the organization can achieve _____, thereby helping them realize their needs of_____."

In attempting to answer these questions, great conversations can be had, which may unpack deeper ideas, it may expand the design hierarchy, there's many benefits to coaching OI. !

An idea may cascade into many levels of ideas.

The point of innovating in the Success Journey is that without introducing a solution with a feature mapping to the employee's needs, the purpose may be incomplete. Developing a solution that is needed, is really where grit is so important and passion keeps the OI Innovator going. In my startup for example, I worked sometimes 18 hours a day, seven days a week on our app, nothing stopped me, I worked and worked and worked more. As part of an OI Policy, the organization may specify work hours for developing OI, or maybe if there is a reward mechanism in place, the conditions might be that it's done in the OI Innovator's own time. In fact, in startup reality you will have worked more by Tuesday midnight, than what most employees will work in an entire week, and you won't get paid for it, and you will go hungry. Fortunately for OI Innovators there's a salary being paid to them. The most important part of designing a solution is making sure the OI Innovator has understood the organization's Success Journey, starting with *the organization's strategy*. Here, I'm talking about the journey for which the organization is on, and the OI is going to help with. For example, our OI Platform helps OI Innovators with their OI journeys which in steps is, DESIGN, TRANSFORM, SCALE.

OI Coaches and OI Innovators need to go completely right-brained here...which is really tough if you're technical. It was for me, I struggled to understand how to talk about other's needs.

I had to actually interview and try to get a deeper understanding of where their real growth issues were in existing OI approaches.

This user experience concept is used in the most successful of products and services. Obviously software is such an example. The 'journey' metaphor can be used for, as examples, employee engagement, financial month-end closing. How others experience something reveals opportunities for improvement and innovation. OI Can help you understand employee journeys using success as the objective, and DESIGN, TRANSFORM, SCALE as steps in an analysis of where things can be improved, based on existing poor designs. You might ask, "What do you need to be successful? How does that journey look like for you? What are your needs?", and then determine why the current designs, transformations processes and scaling up plans aren't working.

OI Success only has a chance if the user experience is better than what they currently have. OI Coaches can be there to encourage OI Innovators to make great OIs.

This was Steve and Elon's drive. Make it the best! But don't unnecessarily deliver more than what is needed, simplicity is key in OI. Once an OI Innovator has a deeper understanding of the how other employees have experienced the OI in demo form, prototyping can begin. And this will keep innovators awake and intellectually stimulated for a very long time. I can recommend, the Stanford University Design School videos (d.school) to help understand the process of design better. Especially lookup and watch David Kelley and Bill Burnett's talks.

11

TRANSFORM

TRANSFORMATION in OI is about the process of taking a design, and making it real. In many organizations, large and small, this is a challenge. The design could be a new process, budget policy update, system control, anything in the organization can be the focus in OI. Digital Transformation contains many OIs which all help to transform clunky manual processes into digital ones, using for example, ERP technologies (at the very least). The book 'Digital Core' explains that for every real-world occurrence, there is the potential for a digital twin. This presents opportunities for new products and services. Consider that for practically everything in the world, there is a digital twin waiting to be invented. Recent digital strategies are looking at how the Internet of Things, Internet of All Things, AI and Robotics are technologies that can drive massive OI, with first-movers potentially getting the advantage over competitors.

But, to keep it practical for now, the key about OI, is

prototyping - please start small and simple, and test it. Build on your lessons - this simple approach will create a wormhole for your ultimate success and save you time, money and an inflamed tail-bone from too much sitting, trying to build a warp-drive, when all the employee needed was a ladder. Agile Project Management basically says the same thing. Get the requirement, sprint to build it, then show and take the feedback, repeat. What it doesn't do is tell you how to approach employees, DESIGN solutions to solve the real problems, TRANSFORM an idea into reality, nor, how to SCALE.

OI Primarily focusses on the essence of transformation. What are you transforming? Elon Musk's biggest transformation that he had to address is building a car factory. Seems he liked that challenge and went on to start the Giga Factory. He often talks about the challenge of Tesla being, not designing the best car in the world, but building the machine (factory) to produce millions of cars, and trucks.

His other business, SpaceX is arguably different, where there, the biggest change he has to address is lowering the price of improved and cheaper space technology and also build a comparatively low-production facility.

Real transformation is generally the combination of action and managing the impact of that action. For example, the transformation of moving to 'Sustainable Transport' (Tesla) requires:

[ACTION 'Design Electric Car' + IMPACT 'Build Factory'].

Simple right? Let's see where it gets more tricky. The change, ie build factory:

[ACTION 'Build Factory' + IMPACT Consume Funds']

and now the change is Consumption of Funds:

[ACTION 'Consume Funds' + IMPACT 'Raise Funds']

In an OI, we have to consider the transformation we are making, and the actions and impact chain we need to manage, to make that change happen. If you recall, the whole notion of an OI is creating transformation in other people's life so they can achieve their success. OIs are half about the preparation needed to get your OI ready for others, and half actually getting them ready for it. OIs are different from, for example typical project management, where only the actions are considered, ie, build an ERP system, the impacts are seen as someone else's problem.

All impacts of all actions are not considered in project plans. This one of the reasons we exclude Project Management in OI, but in its place, we introduce something else: 'Business Actions'.

In OI, impacts are as important as activities and both are actually part of a single 'Business Action', something the business owns, not a project team. Environmental and social responsibilities expect that project owners will be more aware of the impact of their actions on society and the environment, but mostly, they do not.

The other thing to consider, is that every Transformation Action and Transformation Impact, paired as a Business Action, can have chains of sub-activities related to either completing some action AND addressing some impact. Every action, has an impact - find out what they are, whether they are a pain or a gain and to who, and what's involved to ensure they are ready and what that effort will cost - think total Business Case : 'ACTION + IMPACT', this rolls up to the OI Business Case and feasibility.

12

SCALE

You're making great progress in understanding the best-kept secrets of Silicon Valley.

Let's reflect on what you've learned, including this chapter:
1. Coaching OI
2. Success Journey - of the Employee
3. DESIGN with empathy
4. TRANSFORM idea to reality
5. SCALE up within the organization

Now let's look at this final stage of the OI Value Chain : How to SCALE.

Recall the three steps of the OI Value Chain?

>>> **DESIGN, TRANSFORM, SCALE.**

The process of DESIGN and the TRANSFORM Business Actions are completely irrelevant if there is no value, measured in use of the OI by the organization. SCALE value comes from scaling the product or service into the organization. SCALE Plans are clear lists of planned, multiple, SCALE up efforts, growing in numbers of users, with clear details about how the value, according to the employee's needs, will be realized. OI is about by solving employee's problem, in a way that creates additional value for the organization. Win-Win.

>>> **This ensures organizational relevance**

Employees creating value also contribute to your bottom-up business case.

When you use the SCALE approach, you are forced to get to the detail where the real value is unlocked in the SCALE Plans, where a specified number of employees will generate specific value, culminating in SCALE value, per plan or for the whole OI.

So sure, start with big numbers, top-down, but ask yourself...how are you going to get there? Keep on drilling down, till you have specific details about how you will exactly succeed in getting employees to use the OI, at the different scales of usage. Call your shortest and most detailed Scale, the Beta Scale (first tested, working product).

The degree to which you can scale, is the number of, and degree of, success of, the SCALE Plans.

SCALE PLANS (Example):

<u>OI Number XXXXXX</u>
Beta Scale : 3 Beta (Test) Employees
Pilot Scale : 5 Real Employees
<u>OI Release Financial Period 1</u>
Scale Plan 1 : 10 'Friendly' Employees
Scale Plan 2 : 100 Regular US Employees
Scale Plan 3 : 1000 Regular Global Employees
<u>OI Release Financial Period 2</u>
<u>Etc.</u>

Link it directly to your OI Number XXXXXX 'OI TRANSFORM' record as part of your Beta and Pilot Scales, as there won't be any value created yet, so the TRANSFORM budget needs to cover costs. Then plan financial period 1 (in weeks, months or years), assuming a successful Pilot Scale. Determine where exactly you will roll your OI out, who exactly (teams, departments) will you be helping.

This will ensure your business case continuously calibrates with reality. This is something that the OI value-chain is built on and needs, in order to be effective, feasibility needs continuous checking as new costs and value arise.

Be clear about the characteristics of the people who will use the OI, the OI value-proposition to them (Pain-Relievers, Gain Creators, Job Helpers) and of course the financial aspects, because without that, you're not going to generate targeted financial reports, and without that, you are not going to be able to keep your investment business case on track. With your Scale Plans, really aim to create impact value. Clayton Christensen, HBS Professor, tells us that in order to have high impact value, we have to either make something really, really cheap, or introduce something to a new market, who didn't have it before. Make a difference, change the world for your organization. For example, using a cheap cardboard disk in place of an expensive blood dialysis machine (Manu Prakash) is an innovation that disrupted how low-budget clinics analyze blood samples. Generic drug manufacturers bring drugs previously too expensive, to people who can now afford them. His Scale Plans save babies by tens of thousands.

So getting back to tickyRing (the movie ticket holder we introduced as an example innovation), you can communicate via a website, educate through a video, and train through the same video perhaps. Regardless of content, to change people you have to communicate, educate and train - in that order. Assessing where they are after each step is important. Make sure each step is timely and comprehensible, in relation to their need. This approach is especially important in organizations and the right process to follow to do Organizational Change Management. The SCALE Plan, employees adopting the OI to do their job, is about detailed planning of who you are going to help, how, with what OI, communication, education and training content, and the associated costs and revenues, or savings in the case of efficiency savings. Your first 100 users, 1000 users, 10,000 users are your Scale Plans. These scales, measured in value by profits/losses /savings roll-up to your OI Feasibility business case, your ultimate pitch, which needs to be continuously updated and reports sent to shareholders, or executive management in the case of internal organizational innovations. Next we'll learn about how to Coach the OI Value Chain of DESIGN, TRANSFORM, SCALE, in organizations. This is in two parts, principles of OI Management, and then practical frameworks and approaches to start doing OI at OI Clients as part of your OI Practice, or within your organization.

13

MAKING 'IT' HAPPEN

"Just one more thing…"
Steve Jobs

A good friend of mine, an investment banker seasoned in the Valley's antics tells his adult kids "Don't fuck it up". He learned this expression from a Silicon Valley legend, Bill Campbell. A great book about him, 'Trillion Dollar Coach ' portrays Bill as Silicon Valley's most admired Business Coach. In that book, there's an entire chapter dedicated to his famous expression and so I thought it important to do the same. He used to say that all the time. Because, to achieve greatness, you have to get serious. When it comes to making it happen, that is probably the most important thing to keep in mind. Once your pitch is accepted, and budget starts flowing to fund the OI, to keep the OI on the numbers, is the priority for the OI Innovator. If it is the wrong track, take note, list the lessons learned and change track, or 'pivot', until you nail it. Stick to the feasibility numbers. Do what you have to do, to comply with the feasibility report plan. Control feasibility variance, set the target and work to the goal - the numbers.

>>> *Don't fuck it up!*

This is where it's so important to drill down into the corporate strategy and the underlying intentions. Corporate strategy owners will <u>NOT</u> connect with your OI's objectives, only with their <u>OWN strategy</u>, and that's where you have to live, sleep breathe, to keep your numbers on track, and keep the OI delivering, against the organization's objectives.

When I excitedly shared news of our new brand, an 'over-pivot' in my Silicon Valley journey, with seasoned startup coach and friend, she advised, don't confuse people with your what you're doing, stick to the sentence where you're serving the other, the employee, or the strategy owner.

I was completely messing up the message to people, I was still in 'I' mode "Look what I designed", "Look what I did". I still hadn't woken up to the real secret of the Valley, it's not about the brand, it's about what it does for the other - start with that! So in making it happen, you will have to communicate with a lot of people, in the context of their objectives, never your own, or that of the OI. The difference between success and failure, WITH COMPLETE STRANGERS who are NOT EMOTIONALLY connected with you, is to work with their needs, without confusing them with your own needs. Like it or not, strangers don't care about you, they care about what you can do for them - so in making it happen, you've got to start with the other. Implement OI processes, manage OI processes, report on the numbers and stay on track, whatever that takes. If the OI Prototype isn't working or if the messaging is wrong, pivot if you have to. Just keep ensuring that feedback continuously guides the product and the messaging.

14

SILICON VALLEY MENTORS

It's really difficult to stay on the numbers, to not mess things up. This is why mentors, heroic leaders, inspiring pioneers and Silicon Valley investors are so important to learn from in order to start and scale your business. I wanted to introduce different types of hero mentors and leaders some of the best the valley have (or had), people who have guided and coached founders and large business CEO's, to incredible levels of success. Besides, you could not be expected to understand fully what has been written in this book, unless you understood and had examples of how the Success Journey has been used. These heroes understood the Success Journey principles and applied them to their leadership and coaching roles. These are examples of giants, upon whose shoulders, so many of the modern Silicon Valley heroes have stood on. The GSV's Hall of Fame inductees inspire this chapter. Large corporations could learn a lot from these people too, and may have their own heroes.

Larry Sonsini

Larry is a counsel to tech titans. Ideas can be copied, partnerships can be botched, investment deals can go sideways, quick. He's the goto guy to make sure none of this stuff happens. He has been a special advisor to Steve Jobs, Elon Musk, Google, HP and many others. He is one of the most respected people in Silicon Valley. Whilst he is a lawyer, he goes so much further in building relationships of care and integrity. He's the guy who gets deals done, properly.

Dick Kramlich

Dick is a trailblazer in the Venture Capital arena in Silicon Valley. His understanding of people, software and investing proves he's a role model in Silicon Valley. He really helps to nurture founders. Even competitors admire and respect how he makes business decisions combining deep technical understanding and recognizing the potential of founders. At 80 years old he's still a wonderful source of industry knowledge and very much involved in supporting and building founders and portfolios. He is most well known for his integrity.

Bill 'Coach' Campbell (Read Trillion Dollar Coach!)

Bill had such a deep background in Silicon Valley, he is easily recognized as the biggest name in Silicon Valley CEO circles. He has helped Apple, Google in the early days, in fact, there are few big Silicon Valley successes that do not have his direct influence somewhere. He is the ultimate coach to CEOs and founders. Investors and founders speak of him with such deep esteem, it is likely no other person gets as much recognition, as being a mentor in developing some of the best business leaders in the world.

Diane Green

Diane's courage to think different started virtualization at VMWare which is now the bedrock of cloud computing, globally. A pretty big impact on the world! She led VMWare to be one of the biggest software companies globally. She inspires founders to think different, to speak truthfully and not be shy to take big steps into unknown territories.

Mike Homer

Mike played major technology leadership roles in Silicon Valley's software world. From building Netscape, to developing the world's most recognized software technologies. Some say he was the person who set the bar in what software was capable of, and inspired so many to reach that bar. He is described as being incredibly caring of people, but always driving people to push the limits of software. Crazy smart, he would always do the right thing for the people around him.

Ken Coleman

Ken participates on numerous boards even in today's Silicon Valley. He pioneered mentoring in tech startups and has led many himself. He is considered one of the most genuinely caring people in Silicon Valley and is such an iconic hero people speak of him as one of the valley's greats. Specializing in sales and service, he led one of the toughest areas of business in such a way as to be the example of how to tackle the most difficult area of startups, getting customers.

Andy Grove

Andy essentially, led Intel into its biggest growth period ever, setting records for businesses around the world. He grew intel from $4 Billion a year, to over $200 Billion a year. He is considered the best business leader of all time.

Gordy Davidson

Gordy is considered the best of trusted advisors in the area of public offerings. He has taken all the Silicon Valley greats from privately owned to public. He has worked on the biggest mergers in the valley too. He took WhattsApp to Facebook for $19 Billion - the largest acquisition of a private company, of all time. Given the fact that Silicon Valley is a hotbed of investing for the sake of exits as either public or mergers, he is loved for his ability to make people wealthy. He is known as the guy to trust.

Carol Bartz

Carol blazed into the Silicon Valley scene as an executive at Sun Microsystems and CEO of AutoDesk, turning it into one of the most profitable companies in the valley.

Did you notice...

Raising your level of consciousness as someone who passionately wants to achieve 30X growth, would do well to comprehend how these people thought, how they treated others, the behavior they exhibit. Insofar as I can tell, they reflect the very highest levels of consciousness possible in business. Their functional value may easily be comparable to many others. What made them heroes to so many others, was not what they knew, but how much interest and care they had had in other people's Success Journeys. In a sense they are the real ambassadors of the Success Journey story.

15

SILICON VALLEY HEROES

The mentors mentioned previously are just some of the names today's startup founders had, to lean on for guidance and mentoring. It's important to understand also, that Silicon Valley is not just about tech, it's a lot about people. Silicon Valley is experienced as a very difficult place to be successful. Issues such as diversity make it more so, and when talking about pioneers, we need to also acknowledge people who pioneer aspects of society in the Valley.

Their dollar value grows every day...

Sheryl Sandberg

Financial Worth 1.61 billion USD

Sheryl is a big deal, I mean a really big deal. For starters her boss is Mark Zuckerberg and she runs arguably one of the biggest operations, for one of the most well-known brands on the planet. As COO for Facebook, she has fought gender discrimination and won. She also wrote a great book, inspiring millions of women around the world. 'Lean In' sold 140,000 copies in its first week. That's insane! Not only is she an amazing boss and author, but also a speaker. She always draws a large crowd and is one of the valley's biggest inspirations, for all.

Mark Benioff

Financial Worth $ 5 billion USD

Mark got into cloud-computing and made it famous long before anyone else. The challenge with cloud is security, privacy, connection reliability, amongst others. When he started Salesforce with co-founder Parker Harris, he fought the odds with a vision so strong, that it broke the mold of on-premise enterprise solutions. He is a strong advocate for diversity and is an admired and trusted business leader. His staff number 25,000 and the Salesforce head office in San Francisco City is really nice. His showmanship and absolute positive focus makes him a great business leader. He held Steve Jobs in the highest regard, as an inspiration and mentor.

Hasso Platner
Financial Worth 13.7 billion USD

Hasso is one of the founders of SAP, originally a German startup, it transferred to the US, where Hasso has been extremely active in Silicon Valley since early 2000's. His name is on the Stanford University Design School, the very institution that spread 'design-thinking' around the world. His work in Silicon Valley shows he's still a very active founder and has been driving change within SAP's architecture for some time. Always looking for ways to help business run better using SAP software.

SAP Is the largest provider of ERP Business Software, in the world. His CEO, Bill McDermott is worth a study too, and has just resigned. Let's see what Bill does next!

Elon Musk

Financial Worth 19.7 billion USD

Elon to me, epitomizes the startup founder. He sets himself solid missions, develops visions to achieve that purpose and leads execution like very few other founders and CEO's can. He arguably co-founded Tesla, certainly was responsible for building it into one of the most admired businesses in the world. He started SpaceX, vastly reducing the cost of space transportation and has set a goal to lead humanity, in becoming a multi-planetary species.

He talks casually but very intellectually. Elon will be playing a big role in AI and brain interfacing technology.

Here's an example of his leadership: I noticed a Tesla customer complaining to him on twitter, that other Tesla customers were abusing car charging bays by parking in them, to avoid driving around full parking areas, looking for parking. He was pretty angry about this, and later that day I saw him in the Palo Alto city hall parking garage assessing who was parking in the Tesla charging bays. He likes to solve problems asap. If you're interested, Ashlee Vance, one of my coffee machine colleagues in Palo Alto, wrote a superb biography about Elon Musk, being one of the few to actually get quality time with Elon to do this.

BTW, Elon played a tiny roll in the second Iron Man Movie, asking Tony Stark to meet about an Electric Car startup.

Elon has a real sense of humor, although less so these days with the risk of AI, he is working hard to get the right controls in place to prevent malicious AI. It makes him pretty nervous.

Mark Zuckerberg
Financial Worth 73.7 billion USD

Founder of Facebook, Mark has more money than he cares to have, which is why he and his wife have started the Chan Zuckerberg Initiative (CZI) to give away 99% of it. His startup history is only a little blurry when you consider just how blurry startup history can be. He has built an awesome company together with Sheryl Sandberg. The Facebook head office is easily one of the most stunning work places I have ever seen. He constantly challenges his teams to do more, to provide a better product.

I accidentally nearly knocked over Mark's 3 year old daughter with a new broom handle I was carrying. Then I saw her alarmed dad, Mark looking at me with a pretty fierce, "Careful, that's my daughter!" look. Feeling like an idiot, I apologized and moved on...just another jeans and t-shirt kinda dad.

Larry Page, Sergey Brin

Financial Worth: Larry $ 49.1 Billion USD, Sergey $ 47.8 Billion

Larry and Sergey are the founders of Google and more recently, Alphabet, a new business that owns Google and invests in new startups.

Alphabet is valued at upwards of $ 600 Billion, at one point in 2016, it was valued at more than Apple, the most valuable company in the world.

These two are sometimes seen around Silicon Valley and when they are, people talk about them like the legends they are. I saw Sergey once and he seemed a cool guy.

Steve Jobs

Financial Worth $ *127 Billion USD

Silicon Valley has a love/hate relationship with Steve. Most love him, those who worked with him don't. With few exceptions, two of them are Apple's head designer, Jony Ivy, and the man who took over from Steve as CEO, Tim Cook.

*At the time of Steve's passing, he was worth around $ 10 Billion. But if he had held onto his Apple shares, instead of selling them when he was 'fired' from Apple, his fortune would be worth $127 Billion now. There is so much on the net about him that you could research. Inspired, I used to sit in an empty property next door to his humble Palo Alto home eating Apples from the trees he planted in front of his house. What can I say? ...I like Apples.

16

SILICON VALLEY INVESTORS

Giving money to somebody on the basis of an idea is fundamentally flawed and whilst if it happens, and rarely it does, it's because the investor is taking a 'spray and pray' approach to investing, hoping one of the investments will make it big time.

There are different types of investors in the valley. For example, institutional investors, like IBM investing in a startup, or internal product. Then there's Venture Capital firms, such as Sequoia Capital. There's Angel Investors such as Ron Conway, there's family trust investment firms, investing on behalf of a wealthy family, and then there are those with cash to spare and the courage to invest in startups.

Probably the most important thing to learn about investment deals, is the stage of the startup and how the investment is done.

Typically, investment deals are talked about using the terms, 'Seed', 'Late Seed', 'Series A, B,C,D' and on a rare occasion 'E Round'.

Marc Andreessen, co-founder of Netscape and Andreesen Horowitz, one of the biggest, if not the biggest Venture Capital firm in the valley, talks about these different investment rounds as risk mitigation strategies. He says that in the seed round, a startup should be building the team, the product and beta-testing, so seed money or seed investment is to remove the obstacles to do that. Series A, should be about getting the first paying customers, A Round funding should be sufficient to get the marketing right and start selling. Series B, and the rest, is all about scaling the business, and the funding to scale.

These investors have a real knack for spotting talented founders with a strong focus on what people legitimately need, they can spot fake needs a mile away! They primarily invest in the market opportunity, not how great a founder is, or how intelligent the product may be. I think there's scope in existing businesses to take the approach of Silicon Valley investors when it comes to budgeting and business cases. It is done to a degree, but could be improved substantially.

Let's look at some of the valley's greatest investors and firms.

Roelof Botha

Financial Worth $ 300 Million USD

Roelof works at Sequoia Capital and owns four Tesla's. Yes, he's a close friend of Elon. They worked together at PayPal, Roelof as CFO. He sits on the boards of most of Silicon Valley's more recent successes, such as MongoDB. He also just recently started playing a more prominent leadership role at Sequoia, where Doug Leone is likely grooming Roelof for CEO position. Sequoia Capital is iconic in the valley. Doug and previous CEO, Michael Moritz, both deserve further studying. Roelof is a really great guy! IMHO Nobody is as smart, has as much money, and more humility and good grace, than him.

Ron Conway
Financial Worth $ 1.5 Billion USD

Ron is described as a 'Super Angel'. He is super connected in the valley and does a lot, meaning, actively gets involved in social development and financially supports many charities in San Francisco. I had the chance to meet him and pitch our app. His team are more focussed on networking apps not so much enterprise apps like ours. I was sent a well mannered regret.

He is the original Silicon Valley Angel Investor.

Peter Thiel

Financial Worth $ 2.6 Billion USD

Peter invested in a lot of the right startups. His own startup experience was together with Elon and Roelof at PayPal where they worked together and succeeded together. He has very strong political convictions, being the biggest rare Silicon Valley supporter of Donald Trump's presidency. He has enormous influence in the valley, perhaps now a little less so because of his Trump alliance.

17

YOUR SUCCESS JOURNEY

Hopefully by now as somebody interested in coaching OI, you have some understanding of what OI is about. You also have some idea of how raising your consciousness can lead to great things, like the Silicon Valley mentors and heroes. You've also seen examples of successful founders, and have a basic understanding of how investment works and some names and firms to research. They all have great educational video appearances on youtube.

  Let's remind ourselves the essence of the OI Value Chain. It has only 3 'steps' to it.

>>> ***DESIGN > TRANSFORM > SCALE***

Have a look at advice some of the biggest names in Silicon Valley give when answering questions on how to succeed in startups. Their advice follows exactly the OI Value Chain steps. Here's a few examples:

Steve Jobs : "People with passion can change the world for the better."

DESIGN - people with passion, better
TRANSFORM - change
SCALE - the world

Larry Page : "You have to combine both things: invention and innovation focus, plus the company that can commercialize things and get them to people".

DESIGN - invention and innovation focus
TRANSFORM - the company
SCALE - commercialize things and get them to people

Elon Musk : "...try and come up with a demonstration of whatever product or service it is and ideally take that as far as you can. Just see if you can sell that to real customers and start generating some momentum."

DESIGN - try and come up with
TRANSFORM - take that as far as you can
SCALE - see if you can sell that...start generating some momentum

There are many quotes from incredibly successful Silicon Valley legends, they all say the same thing.

DESIGN, TRANSFORM, SCALE

Now it's time to start your own Success Journey by focussing on the needs of others. Here's your Value Chain!

Figure out with data, what do people need/want!

>>> *NAIL IT AND SCALE IT!*

Start your OI Value Chain with the following exercise using a real situation.

DESIGN

> Who am I designing for?

_____

What is their Purpose (Mission)?

_____

_____

_____

_____

What is their game-plan (Vision)?

_____

_____

_____

What is the strategy they need help with?

What is the strategic goal they need help with?

What is the strategic NEED they need help with?

Design and describe the first solution

Draw:

Describe

_____

_____

_____

_____

TRANSFORM

Describe what the transformation is, that will develop the solution and manage the impacts.

_____

_____

_____

_____

PLANNED COST_____

Describe impacts to manage, in developing the solution.

_____

_____

_____

PLANNED COST_____

SCALE

Describe how you would test and pilot the solution in a real world situation.

_____

_____

_____

_____

PLANNED COST_____

Describe how you would get your employee onboard.

_____

_____

_____

PLANNED COST   _____

PLANNED REVENUE   _____

PLANNED PROFIT   _____

Describe how you would get your first 10 paying customers.

_____

_____

_____

_____

_____

PLANNED COST   _____

PLANNED SAVINGS/REVENUE _____

PLANNED PROFIT   _____

Describe how you would get your first 100 paying customers.

_____

_____

_____

_____

PLANNED COST   _____

PLANNED REVENUE   _____

PLANNED PROFIT   _____

INVESTMENT BUSINESS CASE

TAM_____

SAM_____

SOM_____

TRANSFORMATION COSTS (From idea to reality)

PROJECT COST_____

IMPACT COSTS_____

TOTAL PROFITS FROM SALES_____

LESS TOTAL TRANSFORMATION COSTS_____

TOTAL PROFIT_____

ROI : COSTS (INVESTMENT) / PROFITS

ROI : _____ / _____

RATE OF RETURN:
ROI / #YEARS

=_____

GO AHEAD?   YES, OR START AGAIN

(IF IT WAS EASY, EVERYBODY WOULD BE STINKING RICH!)

18

COACHING OI

>>> *Every manager in every organization in the world could consider coaching OI in their team.*

Management students are taught that the four functions of management are: Plan, Lead, Organize and Control. I've altered this a little to be more aligned to managers who want to be OI Coaches. Let's look at an idea that all managers could coach OI, as part of becoming better leaders. I think that the following are the good key functions of any modern manager:

1. **Strategize** (SWOT Analysis & Mapping)
2. **Lead** (Mission, Vision, Culture, Motivation)
3. **Transform** (Transcend+Transition)
4. **Coach** (Supporting people to keep strategic)

If we remember, that OI follows the OI Value Chain, DESIGN, TRANSFORM, SCALE, then a manager, while coaching OI, would be encouraged to learn that their role, and this applies to startups and big business, is to help their team to 'Manage' each part of the OI Value Chain.

Each part of the OI Value Chain requires strategizing, leadership, transformation and coaching.

	DESIGN	TRANSFORM	SCALE
Strategize	1.1 Activities	2.1 Activities	3.1 Activities
Lead	1.2 Activities	2.2 Activities	3.2 Activities
Transform	1.3 Activities	2.3 Activitiies	3.3 Activities
Coach	1.4 Activities	2.4 Activities	3.4 Activities

Coach OI Matrix

The table above is a simple matrix approach to understanding what needs to be done in managing OI Value Chain activities. We'll introduce each step in the following pages. **Please note**, if this chapter appears confusing, it's because it is better represented in a matrix, not linear as it appears in the following paragraphs. Have a look at CoachOI.com for the Coach OI Matrix where it is presented in a better way. This section is useful to read, but not intended to assist you achieving a full understanding.

1. DESIGN

1.1 DESIGN : Strategize

Here, coaching OI covers what we talked about earlier in this book, introducing you to strategy. In coaching OI, we get to understand what the mission of the employee is about, what their vision and strategies are. In doing so, strategic needs surface, being things they need to achieve their objectives, not the organization's objectives. This is what we call strategizing, as you will be working with your potential OI Innovator around their strategy, perhaps offering opinions on things where the coaching OI will mean having data-driven insights to offer. Enterprise systems can provide great data, and through analysis of this data, OI Coaches can gather insights, about things that might be of value to the employee.

1.2 DESIGN : Lead

In discussing what leadership is, you may find thousands of books on the subject and there are a lot of design-thinking 'experts'! I choose to follow a leadership theory, that the most legitimate leader, is one that cares for and helps to grow their people. This approach for me, is the most ethical, and human approach I have found, and resonates with the

Coaching concept. I have pursued an understanding of leadership for 30 years, and this one works for me. You may find another one that works for you. Regardless, the approach you take in leading in the design part of a manager's job, you need to provide a context that will result in the best execution of design possible. The most important component of which, is empathy. So create a leadership style that enhances empathy and gives empathy the space it needs to do its work, when helping OI Innovators designing new ways of working.

1.3 DESIGN : Transform

Design-thinking is probably the best way to execute the design function when coaching OI. Transcend the ego and empathize, strategize, then transition to design-thinking. There's plenty to learn from David Kelley and Bill Burnett. Youtube has many of their talks, I think it would be worthwhile to learn from them.

1.4 DESIGN : Coach

Coaching is incredibly empowering for people that have a growth mind-set and give others permission to coach them. The important aspect of coaching is to seek permission first, to coach, from either the team or individual. With data in hand, giving feedback on the execution of the design work, helps teams and individuals grow, by reminding them of the strategy, and keeping them aligned to both the organizational strategy, but driven by their own strategy to succeed. Accountability, as part of execution can be harsh, people get fired for not executing according to plan. Coaching is a way of helping to improve execution performance, without the pressure of being at the coal face. A lot can be learned about coaching online. Bill Campbell is in my opinion, the best example of a business coach. On CoachOI.com we have a few videos of Bill. Coaching specifically, in relation to executing design work, relates to unpacking the needs and empathy process. Feedback about how the OI Innovator and other employees felt through the process of identifying the real problems, to developing a prototype, what was their experience? Did the team members really dig down deep into the problem, were the OI Innovators really listening? These are the things OI Coaches attempt to understand in being able to coach the individual OI Innovator through the Design step, with the team.

2 TRANSFORM

2.1 TRANSFORM : Strategize

Strategizing how to transform an idea into reality, takes doing an analysis of the strengths and weaknesses of your team, in relation to what has to be done. We tend to go directly to technical or functional competencies here, when what is more important, many believe is how the team will work together. Transforming an idea into reality is easy, transforming an idea into reality well, is extremely challenging. Just ask Elon Musk, who had to build a car factory, in order to transform his idea of an electric vehicle into reality. Transformation involves Business Actions, so identifying what strengths a team has in executing on actions, and where weaknesses will result in risks, executing Business Actions, are the things that come into focus, while managing the OI TRANSFORMATION step.

2.2 TRANSFORM : Lead

The approach to leadership in managing transformation execution is a little different to leadership in the design process. Leading transformation requires a real good understanding of the organizational context, agendas of key stakeholders, executive processes etc., thus being able to think ahead in terms of predicting risks and issues. Generally, a risk relates to the Business Actions, in other words, what needs to be done. An issue relates to a person, or group of people. So a *risk* of some 'thing' required for the transformation to happen not being delivered in time, is that the Business Action completion date could be affected. Whereas, the *issue* of people not wanting to use that same 'thing' is an issue that should have been thought of ahead of time, for example. Internal team strife creates its own set of issues and leaders know how to prevent risks and issues by being proactive, and caring for and helping their people to grow.

2.3 TRANSFORM : Transform

Transcend 'power and control' mindset. Transition to efficient execution, which starts with a Business Action list, based on what came out of strategizing activities. A simple 'flightpath' would be a good start, relaying the high-level plan with stakeholders will help unearth some incorrect assumptions, and reveal risks and issues that may affect the execution. With a revised, improved and agreed flightpath, detailed Business Action scheduling can begin. The objective of this Business Action schedule, is to deliver a usable, tested OI, ready for employee 'beta' testing. So the architecting, developing, prototyping, testing will have been done, and ready for a 'friendly' team to try it out. When the friendly team provides feedback, and the iterative cycles produce a minimum viable product, in other words the simplest product, an employee is willing to use, then wider employee group can begin using it, but still in beta testing mode.

2.4 TRANSFORM : Coach

In coaching OI, having data at this point, about how the OI Innovator, leading the team has been experienced by the team, can be useful. And vice versa, how the OI Innovator felt about the performance of the team. The execution of the Business Actions can be discussed and ways to improve, agreed. Also the quality of the OI delivered as a beta OI, is it up to expectations and will it solve the problem that the employees/teams have?

3. SCALE

3.1 SCALE : Strategize

The first SCALE Plan we talk about is the 'Beta Scale' then

'Pilot Scale'. When that's successful, then look at the first 10 employees that might use the OI, then the next 100 and so on. The SCALE Plans detail how to SCALE up through the employee community that might use the OI. Looking at employee's strategic needs, and then deliver targeted:

1) Communication, 2) Education, 3) Training. The result of this stage, is determining what kind of content and platforms would provide the best chance of the employees agreeing to a beta test. In order to truly scale, the product must be either incredibly cheap to the department or team, OR bring some new NEEDED functionality to employees and/or the team, who didn't have it before. There might be a number of Scale Plans as a result of this stage, from a Beta Scale to possibly, four or five Scale Plans, one being 10,000 employees in month 3 for example. If you evolve your product or service, then you might link the Scale Plans to your latest product version or service version.

3.2 SCALE : Lead

There's many ways to sell, essentially, that's what we're doing here. It all relates to how the OI Innovator wants to develop relationships with the potential OI Stakeholders. I can only say that for me, sales is a lot more rewarding, when I really find meaningful engagement with my client, hearing their needs and delivering solutions to those needs, where permission is given. Coaching OI is about encouraging the OI Innovator to build work relationships which are crucial for OI success. The power of informal networks in the organization can never be underestimated. There are easy ways, be charming, flirtatious, fickle, but I don't think these create sustainable sincere relationships. In OI the relationship with stakeholders needs to be sincere, when you're disrupting, you have to deeply empathic, it's hard work, but must be done. Steve Jobs said, "If you don't want to be a leader, sell ice cream." I think this means that if you can't be empathic and build real relationships with people who may use the OI, then don't bother with the OI in the first place, because you won't be able to SCALE, people won't want to change from what they're doing. If the OI is truly brilliant in terms of solving a problem, then SCALE is easy.

3.3 SCALE : Transform

Executing disruption is tough! Transcend to an indestructible, positive mindset. Transcend to a mindset of empathy where you can lead with the other's need.
Transition to disciplined SCALE Plans. Raymond Loewy, arguably America's greatest industrial designer said that consumers are torn between a *curiosity* about new things,

and a consumer's *fear* of new things. He reminds us of this point something that we HAVE TO UNDERSTAND WHEN SCALING:

> >>> **You cannot sell something new, with something new, you have to sell it as something familiar with something new or introduce something new with something familiar.**
>
> (Thanks Phil!)

The first Apple computer could be introduced as something new, because it had a keyboard like a typewriter, and a TV, both were familiar to their potential customers. So when creating the market message, in all 3 stages of engaging the potential customer, (Communicate, Educate, Train), introduce the product in such a way as to alleviate sufficiently the chance of people's fear of the new, whilst leveraging their curiosity of the new.

3.4 SCALE : Coach

With data about how successful the SCALE Plan or Plans were, it's good to be able to unpack the lessons. Where 10 employees used the OI, did they use it effectively? That data is useful in providing clues about how to repeat that Scale Plan for the next 100 employees.

Hopefully these introductions to the activities that an OI Leader might be considering, will create further discussion with peers and colleagues. As this is such a new management and business field, we believe that people might need help in becoming OI Coaches, which is why we have a global network of people who develop OI Coaches within organizations.

19

A SILICON VALLEY MINDSET

Data that shows a path to opportunity, is exciting to people with the right mindset (7-15% of people have this mindset). So if you want a large enterprise to think different, then read on. The rest of this book is about getting enterprises to think and work like a Silicon Valley startup, no matter how big (or small).

When you get employees with the OI Mindset together as a team, focussed on the opportunity data (where there's problems or opportunities in the organization), then applying the principles and practices in this book and creating an OI Culture can make a difference. Creating an OI Community in a larger organization is about working with the 7-15%, the employee segment who are 'naturally occurring' innovators that exist in the organization and will exist across multiple business functions. When you can profile these people, through for example surveys and interviews, gather these people into a community with clear goals and the opportunity data, you can then create OI Teams that can easily work across business functions, especially important when bringing an OI to life. OI Teams are better if the members are from diverse fields and in terms of backgrounds, the more the diverse, the better the design, ask David Kelley.

We also focus on the idea that OI can happen anywhere within an organization improving business areas like policies, systems, processes etc. as well as, with the products or services they market, sell, make and deliver.

> >>> ***The biggest value we can get from Silicon Valley isn't products like Google or Facebook, but rather, the way they work as organizations.***
> ***That's what this book is about!***

Get OI 'Step One' certified, free at:

CoachOI.com

Part Three

Coach OI

20

AESOP HAD THE RIGHT IDEA

A Fable - The Old Farmer

An elderly farmer, whose children were constantly bickering about who should own the family farm in the future, gathered them together and presented a bundle of sticks tied up with rope. The elderly farmer said that whoever could break the bundle of sticks in half, could claim ownership of the farm. They all tried breaking it over their knees and their backs, none could, they gave-up. The farmer then untied the bundle and gave one stick to each child. They each broke their own stick with ease, thereby all gaining ownership and responsibility for, the farm.

This Aesop fable supports the underlying principle of *real* OI. No single person can 'own' or 'do' the OI. But if everyone has ownership of the OI the chances of success increase tremendously.

Remember this fable and think about the wisdom of the approach - as outlined in this book. When we're doing OI, we will do the same, just like the wise farmer separating the bundle of sticks and encouraging everyone to do a little to achieve a lot.

As we go through the rest of this book we will uncover a simple tried and tested practical approach to Coach OI and assisting organizations to become 'OI Active', anywhere in the world.

21

THE PURPOSE OF COACHING OI

Earlier in this book it was suggested that Coaching OI is about evolving management thinking from the functions of Plan, Lead, Organize, Control to Strategize, Lead, Transform, Coach.

Old		New
Plan	⇒	Strategize
Lead	⇒	Lead
Organize	⇒	Transform
Control	⇒	Coach

When coaching OI we use these functions as enablers of the DESIGN, TRANSFORM, SCALE, OI Value Chain. At first, coaching OI might involve assisting the manager of a department to develop these skills, then the manager would effectively start coaching OI themselves, identifying and helping would-be OI Innovators in their team. Introducing how to go about coaching OI to all managers in an organization, is about introducing a set of processes. First step in doing this, is for Senior OI Coaches, to do Success Journey sessions with all the managers, identifying which of them are the natural innovators. This will be a selection of 7-15% of them, hopefully more. The Success Journey session with them will have resulted naturally, in them making clear that they really want to assist their team to become more innovative. In this situation, coaching OI can be really powerful.

The right type of manager will welcome the support. At this point, someone experienced in coaching OI, for example an OI Practice Lead, can explain that OI offers a journey for the manager, that will aim to facilitate transcending how the selected managers see their roles in an organization, from functional head, to leading a function and coaching OI. When that happens across the organization, then we get a truly innovative culture, then we can disrupt markets with great products and services, because 7-15% of employees are OI Innovators and know what it means to innovate and respond to needs. Once the natural innovators are on board and doing OI, then the early adopters can be addresses, with the assistance of the new OI Coaches. Later, the 'late adopter' managers, and even maybe some of the 'laggard' managers. OI Can happen at many levels of the organization with varying degrees of problem-solving OIs within an organization. For OIs to be effective, they begin at a strategic level. Every department or team has a strategic level, it just depends on how well the strategic level is leveraged within the team as a way to guide the team, being always cognizant of the team's strengths and weaknesses, and how those map to the team's opportunities and threats. I'd suggest that organizational change which is not innovation-driven, is basically change for change-sake, which is why we hardly mention managing change in this book, but we do see change management being necessary within the OI Value Chain and see managing change as part of the OI processes, but within a strategically meaningful context. We hope people who are Change Managers today will become Senior OI Coaches and OI Practice owners in the future.

Strategizing includes a SWOT analysis which is about developing innovative ways to leverage on organizational strengths to achieve an outcome. Conversely, it's about devising innovative risk response plans to mitigate threats. In both instances this could be a product, service, restructuring, or any combination of scenarios which provides a solution that helps the organization take advantage of a market opportunity or mitigate a market threat. When an organization finds itself in a position where external or internal dynamics create challenges to corporate performance, then OI is required, resulting in a new way of doing business, with new products or services, for internal or external customers. This new way can be realized through the process of OI, to achieve transformation, such as for example in Digital Transformation projects and strategies.

This OI product or service could be a new information system for internal and external stakeholders, better-educated employees, more effective business processes or work-flows, a new solution for a new market, as examples. This new product or service will likely bring about the need for a new way of doing business. These needs, solutions and changes can only be identified and managed using *diligent* Strategic OI to achieve improved corporate performance. If OI is not done, then the organization will carry on the trajectory of its current state, as opposed to achieving the 'D*esired State'* (Lewin, 1951). This is akin to the 'Innovator's Dilemma' (Christensen). Strongly opposed to the idea of nuclear weapons, Einstein, in 1946 said that we cannot solve our problems with the same thinking we used when we created them. That's why OI is designed to be different and can be scaled in organizations, implemented in every department and organization around the world. This will achieve a different way of thinking. Don't keep using a hammer just because it's the only tool in the toolbox - get new tools, like OI whose objective is continuous business growth through solving the organization's problems AND internal efficiency and effectiveness problems, using radical solutions. This will help the organization become better at solving the world's real problems.

Origins of *People* Change Management in Business

Change Management was the label given by early western management theorists during and after, the Industrial Revolution. Practitioners would manage initiatives whose focus was to improve business performance. These Industrial Revolution management specialists began to understand that people *(NOT only new technology)*, were the essential link to greater productivity and profitability. In many ways, we have forgotten these lessons and possibly many incorrectly believe that the solution to performance problems is to crack the whip or pull out a check book, buying either new people or better technology. This implies the importance of culture as the primary enabler of growth. (Yes, for OI to work, the right culture needs to be developed.)

As a result of studying the link between group productivity and the working environment, Organizational Change Management became a *methodical* process for achieving new and better ways of conducting business - without necessarily spending vast amounts of money. This positive link between Organizational Change Management and better profitability highlighted the value of effective Organizational Change Management, a long time ago.

The management field of improving organizational performance from a people perspective was given the title 'Organizational Development' (OD) in the 1950's . The field focused on two aspects, (i) how business activities were done, and (ii) how people could be managed to do these things quicker, better and smarter. Kurt Lewin was a German-American psychologist, one of the modern pioneers of social, organizational, and applied psychology . He was one of the first to study group dynamics and foster concepts that became the foundation for Organizational Development. Lewin introduced two key terms underpinning these studies – concepts he called 'Action Research' and 'Group Dynamics'. Through various evolutionary steps in management thinking, OD has become more people-oriented with concepts such as "Learning Organization" (Peter Senge). And similarly, Change Management has come to mean the people-side of change, whereas Organizational Change Management relates to managing all changes physical and otherwise in the organization. Often this involves people and then Change Management is used to assist changing the hearts and minds of people, in relation to the broader organizational change initiative and associated real-world changes driven by 'Action Research' (Business policy, process re-engineering, technology etc.)

Organizational Development (OD)

Within the context of departmental responsibility, OD's strategic targets (as part of the HR department), for example, could be the percentage of workforce that have taken part in self-mastery programs. Although these OD programs do contribute to the sustainability and good health of an organization, they are not necessarily directly linked to specific strategic objectives and targets outside of HR, such as Earnings Before Interest and Tax (EBIT).

To clarify, an OD intervention can improve the value that employees add to an organization, such as providing them with the understanding of how to become OI Coaches, *whilst* OI is a Value Chain where OI Innovators can be developed to assist enhancing the organization's ability to reach, for example, its shareholder goals. The point is this: Organizational Change Management has often been confused with OD or Change Management. Organizational

Change Management may have been more effective if it had been have been focused on changing business to improve strategic performance, and not be simply an 'HR thing'. Although HR can play a role in training and education, amongst other things, within an executive-driven Change framework. So to clear the confusion, I recommend using the term OI to name the capabilities and resources aimed at improving how business works. Here's a thought:

>>> *Coaching OI is the new Change Management*

Project Managers

Throughout the digital transformation history of forward-looking businesses and economies, Organizational Change Management has been used to change corporate cultures, leadership styles and generally support the process of digital usage as envisioned by the architects of the new technologies, SAP is one such example. Now that much of this green-field digitization has happened, businesses are far more representative of the rich diversity of people, as technology can be learned and used by anyone. However, there's arguable value in always having a focus on simplifying business basics and implementing organizational improvement initiatives, this is something technology cannot do by itself. Which is why Coaching OI can become a sort of 'safe-haven' career, where the job of Coaching OI will likely not be automated in the foreseeable future. Making business run simpler using technology, applies to all kinds of organizations, government, business, and community organizations for example. Organizational Change Management as part of Project Management has been used widely to implement large-scale systems by identifying and reducing people resistance to the change **and** preparing the organization for the new way of *doing* business through a variety of processes. However, new enterprise solutions such as SAP S/4 HANA have a very different approach. SAP Has recognized that in order to stay relevant, it needs to provide a platform for companies to solve their own problems with client-specific digital innovations. So we have to reframe how do corporate change. Modern Organizational Change Management, in the scope of OI, has to change its approach to managing the change brought about by for example SAP S/4 HANA. Additionally, the Project Management approach used in the past is no longer relevant to implementing new technologies, it's not about pushing innovations, it's about supporting employee-driven innovation. Now it's all about OI when implementing new technology in the organization.

I suggest, OI can be be used for the sake of becoming better organizations and serving all stakeholders more effectively, the business case for committing to OI as a key strategic lever. Here's another idea:

>>> *Coaching OI is the new business Project Management*

Coaching OI could be a line-competency of *every* manager in every type of organization, as all OIs can be directly linked to the team's strategic objectives and initiatives.

The number of, and different types of DESIGNS and TRANSFORMATIONS occurring in a single organization can be quite complex – consider the myriad of interdependencies between these DESIGNS and TRANSFORMATIONS. Today, often, individual employees are asked to undertake Business Project responsibilities because 'They have done Change or Project Management before' – this often results in the wrong people being given roles where they have inadequate skills or experience and then fail. They may have been Change Agents or Managers for a Culture Change Program for example, but they may not have been in an implementation project of an Enterprise Resource Planning system (ERP – A business system which enables the business processes for example, SAP). Very often people with limited Change experience are expected to play the same role in any kind of Change Program. A useful analogy is assuming that someone who can drive a car can also fly a helicopter. Many people with limited Change Management consultants market themselves as being Change Consultants or specialists for any kind of Change. The challenge is that different kinds of changes require different kind of Change Management consultants, which is why this book is about Organizational Innovation, not Change Management. OI Requires a specific kind of Change Management specialist, that we call an OI Lead Coach who focusses on developing manager's skills in coaching OI, in and around the organization, whilst as part of the organization's OI Practice, enabling the corporate-wide OI processes. I'm hoping we can evolve specifically-skilled change and project related professionals, into being Senior OI Coaches and OI Practice leaders, internal to the organization, or run private OI Practices that have multiple clients.

Today, due to the popularization of the term 'Change Management', an instruction to the HR or Communications Department from senior management to facilitate an organizational improvement project, is generally given in an attempt to improve the success of a business/IT project, OD intervention or strategic initiative. However, at a strategic management level, Change Management is seldom considered, and very likely the reason organizations fail at transformation. This may be because the full effect and impact of strategic innovations, improvements or objectives are not understood adequately. Could it be that, there's an incorrect assumption that a 'people intervention' or a 'communications plan', on its own, will bring about a real sustainable new way of doing business? In these cases, the process of Change Management is unknown – often a costly mistake indeed. That's why OI is a useful term to encapsulate all that is required when enhancing or improving an organization, or adapting it for new products and services it may be introducing to the market.

OI Could be used to *enable* the process of corporate strategizing, in order to ensure that a measurable and effective Value Chain is in place, thereby reducing the risk of NOT achieving the strategic desired state of being a market leader.

The following example is used to highlight this point:
A Sales VP may argue that higher sales targets requires a larger sales expense budget – but neglects to identify the possibility of using OI as a whole to help the organization become more "Customer-Centric" and not just "Customer-

Focused" - which would improve relationships with customers through more effective processes and systems.

>>> *Corporate Strategy setting is therefore, in itself, the beginning of the OI Value Chain. What is its purpose, game-plan and objectives?*

To develop this point further, wherever there are strategic objectives or targets, there could be an OI Policy in place that will guide the respective stakeholders towards those targets and objectives, using OI to make strategic enhancements, as needed.

Leading OI

Leadership is a key construct of OI. It is often the case that people within the HR department are given the lead role of a business change program, supporting some business objective, IT or otherwise. This may be because top management mistakenly assumes (or is incorrectly informed) that Business Project-driven Change is mostly about changes to job descriptions and/or organizational hierarchy and managing the resistance this brings about. It may also happen that the internal communications department or the marketing division takes on the lead role of Change - once again with top management incorrectly thinking only of one component of Change, i.e. communication. In other instances industrial psychologists are given the job of Change Leader or Manager because of the perceived specialized analysis required to present behavioral models and initiate head-space changes – whilst this is somewhat true, these areas of Change are only parts of sub-components of what is needed to implement changes required to support for example, a Business Transformation Programs (BTP). It is also important that leadership and management of the OI should never be entirely delegated to an 'outsider'.

The most senior accessible manager/executive/business owner MUST lead and manage the Change that corporate-wide improvements bring about. The delegation of the change initiative to a single department or internal/external consultant increases the risk of failure, which results resulting in a 'less-than-desired' outcome and potentially failed transformation.

Time and time again, where strategic OIs are not led by the top available executive, the OI does not realize its initial objectives. The term 'most senior available executive' refers to the highest-ranking executive-oriented employee of that organization who has sufficient time to give the OI the leadership it needs. If it will be a corporate-wide and complex OI, then that highest-ranking employee must prioritize time for the OI with commitments to chair senior OI Lead meetings, specific to the OI in question.

In relation to strategic performance, CoachOI.com provides an OI Platform for management (private, state or non-profit) to manage Strategic OIs and offer from this online platform, OI Coaches to assist with one or more strategic OI identified as an enabler of critical strategic objectives.

Many modern senior organizational lead roles, especially in politics, are often short-lived, so their Change activities focus on managing perception instead of managing the real Change required. Political leaders, organizational top management, and business owners could all benefit by taking on the role of the OI Lead. Real OI requires real OI Leaders – if managers want to be recognized as legitimate OI Leaders, they need to show they can be effective OI Coaches. This means offering more than just a speech or being rhetoric about an initiative – it means actively taking ownership of developing OI Capabilities, as an OI Lead.

People and Change

The basis of modern Organizational Development (OD) is focused on developing people's capability maturity (CMMI). In order to increase the sustainability of OI, it is of the utmost strategic importance that organizations about to implement OI, remember the principles of OD and through the OI Preparation Process, develop planned capability improvement objectives. These capabilities include increasing the maturity of employees to have the mindset to become more value-adding members of the organizational community, than just doing a job. 7-15% Of employees will naturally want to do this. The rest will take more time.

To achieve strategic goals, an organization must invest in its people. OD Is only a framework of trying to get this done effectively, there are useful OD ideas, such as 'The Learning Organization'. Unfortunately, many executives, not aligned to management as a liberal art, treat people as a disposable liability. Employees are continuously at risk of being disposed. By implementing OI, employees can become a lever for success, for at least those who want to *innovate*.

Sadly, for those who don't, it is highly likely their jobs will be automated, as many people as possible are encouraged to become OI Coaches and OI Innovators.

In conclusion, *I hope that this chapter has been confusing for you, because quite frankly, the subject of change management, project management and innovation is totally confused around the world. Maybe it's time for new thinking, time for...*

>>> Coaching OI

Ideas for responses to OI Questions:

A quick answer to the question, "What is OI?"
Organizations always have room for enhanced strategic capabilities in every team and department.
OI helps with that.

A quick answer to "How?"
OI is a way to empower employees, through managers coaching OI, developing natural innovators (7-15% of employees, into Organizational Innovations that enhance the organization's strategic capabilities.

A quick answer to "Can I become coach OI?"
Yes, at CoachOI.com.

22

THE OI PRACTICE LEAD

If OI is not managed properly there is an *extremely* good chance that trying to do *OI will* have adverse effects on a number of critical business performance areas ranging from finance, to credibility with customers, and other stakeholders. Pages of this book could be filled with business cases where proper management of OI has not been done - resulting in substantial business problems.

>>>**But it has to be done.**

Understanding the organization's policies, culture, architecture or business framework is key in understanding the need for an OI Practice within the organization, or at least to have one contracted to the organization. The core of how the organization's revenue is created, products and services are procured, cash is managed etc. must be stable whilst OIs go through the OI Value Chain, and become the new way of doing things. There must be no risk to core business processes. The OI Practice would take accountability for making sure this doesn't happen when introducing a new OI.

One could say that within an organization, the value the organization creates is the convergence point or the 'value-add' equilibrium where *demand* is met with intelligent *supply*, in terms of the service or product provided to customers. The constructs of any organization, being, people, processes and systems - must converge in an optimal arrangement (desired state) in order to produce the optimal 'value-add' equilibrium. The sensitivity of this equilibrium is dependent on macro and micro conditions, some controllable and others not. Needless to say, this convergence point is the key to any organization's success. The right people must know their roles in the business processes and, how to use the systems which enable those processes. People, processes and systems must become one. They must work together as best as possible, in order to achieve value for stakeholders and shareholders alike. Now, with SAP S/4 HANA, businesses can broaden the periphery of optimal equilibrium by responding to a wider range of challenges, quicker, with rapidly deployable innovations on the SAP S/4HANA platform. This reduces the need for classical ERP type Organizational Change Management where stakeholders had to be pushed into a specific set of standardized processes and apps.

An objective of the executive management team, is to embed and enable a measurable, manageable business model and platform for ensuring that the business of meeting omni-channel needs, is consistently improving, through innovation and transformation with an ever *more* intelligent supply chain. OI Helps executives to do this well.

The core business demand/supply equilibrium is the reason for the existence of the business, and there is good profit in extending this core using OI. The value earned from the intelligent supply of goods and/or services is the reason that stakeholders, for example, shareholders take an interest in an organization and provide capital to achieve the mission. OI Focussed on innovating and extending this core, will add value, market-value, resulting in more market-share and share-holder value. This is true for profit-oriented, state-owned or community-based organizations (except the market-value part of course). If this 'value-add' equilibrium fails, there can be catastrophic impacts for all stakeholders. It will fail when demand drops, meaning the products or services have become less relevant to the market that once needed it. Managing OI around a multi-channel, multi-stakeholder, multi-system environment requires a very specific type of OI Practice Leader with a specific skill-set supporting Senior OI Coaches who develop OI Coaches, who in turn enable the OI Value Chain. This is best done using the OIActive.com platform. A digital platform, working with everyone from the least-paid to the most-paid employees. The OI Practice Lead secures the foundation of the organization, the core, whilst providing the arena to do OI, aiming to expand the core. In these times, strategic goals need to be agile, and as such, this arena where OI is encouraged and OI Coaches work, is thought to be most effective, when it is well-known to be a key strategic capability of the organization. Many organizations try and do this with a Project Management Office or PMO. We've discussed some shortfalls of the Project Management approach in business, and recommend an OI Practice taking over, with just a little development of the people in the PMO and some diversity in skillsets.

It's understood this concept is new, but actually maybe it already is in place and might be considered to be the inward-looking Project Portfolio of an organization on one hand, and Change Management on the other. Many believe that change efforts must be directed at only one business construct - that being people. They forget about the business processes and computer systems, which in many cases these days need to be replaced with cross-functional systems and cross-functional processes. In order for cross-functional processes and systems to work well, managers and organizational leaders need to think more *along* the business instead of *within the silos* of the business. The age-old departmental or silo view is still very prevalent in modern business, especially in America. For good reason, those silos may hold tens of thousands of employees...soon to be automated! The future is more likely, if you look at Silicon Valley organizations, going to be, strategically integrated OI teams, and departments replaced by apps. Goodbye silos! And good riddance!! No thanks to the military and religious organizations which inspired them in the first place.

The desired-state for most organizations might be to forget about the age-old concept of departments or even fixed-titles. Silicon Valley organizations have done well to NOT build these structures. Generally, when business processes are designed, they include roles that are unpacked within role definition catalogues and mapped to competencies. Depending on the workload or frequency of transactions within a particular process, people who have been deemed competent to fulfill a role in that process may be be allocated to that role, thereby completing the process within specified performance criteria. The same applies for process controls and segregation of duties within processes. These roles are soon to be automated. Very soon! Many have already been off-shored.

Within agile environments, roles are not used, but rather technical skills, as roles become blurry. Nowadays, these skills are being automated. For example, in the past you may have needed a team of programmers to integrate your systems, now there's Zapier, which automatically does the integration for you, in seconds! And anybody can do it, except may a few who have never used a computer.

Old management theory taught the greatest minds that, organizations must be split up into departments for accountability and other scientific management oriented purposes. The greatest minds are still running some of the greatest organizations like this. But more recently, the greatest Silicon Valley minds are realizing that strategic power lies in developing employees who are, committed to the shared vision and strategic goals, who can work cross-process and cross-role in order to achieve objectives. They want people who understand how to work within multi-channel/stakeholder/system environments, always adding the most value to organizations, they can. These employees are natural OI Innovators. A lack of holistic understanding of an organization's channels, stakeholder and system environment may be the reason that new executives are often a generation or two younger than their existing executive colleagues. There is often such a lack of understanding of systems and cross-functional processes that operational challenges requiring true cross-department collaboration cannot be managed effectively by old-school thinking. This is because large amounts of data are being manipulated manually in spreadsheets by managers, or their departmental spreadsheet ninjas, and then decisions are made on the analysis of these reports. The data being fed into these reports is often highly questionable and is certainly seldom the result of a thorough, disciplined process. Whereas, executives reporting directly out of systems that reflect the true status of transactions and other organizational activities are more reliable. Even better when this is done by the executive, who understands the systems and reports, and not their junior associates, where mistakes can easily be made by staff who don't understand the processes and data.

Relating to the systems construct of the 'value-add' equilibrium, it is unfortunate that generally, senior executives still regard information systems as being modern menaces required for looking at spreadsheets compiled by their personal assistants. They don't really understand that computer systems enable business-processes, governance and corporate performance.

Sadly, this lack of understanding of modern, system-enabled organizational models, often means that their effectiveness as an executive becomes diminished, and they're made redundant. BTW, If this has happened to you, please become an OI Practice Leader, you could really help the organization you're at, or new organizations and it'd be a step forward for your industry, retaining your wisdom, and guidance on building strategic capabilities.

Systems are becoming more cross-functional and less dependent on external manual decision-making. As such, the focus of managers must change to become more aligned to the organization's cross-process and cross-functional business-model requirements.

There is an urgent and serious requirement to up-skill managers at all levels with regard to cross-functional business and system-thinking. They could be encouraged to transcend silo-thinking, which has been the legacy of the past and embrace effective cross-functional business integration.

I think it's worth remembering that the effective convergence of systems, processes and people relies heavily on these three principles working in balance. Leadership of

OIs within an organization must be singular in its objectives and direction, otherwise this balance may become an unmanageable chaotic situation. You cannot extend a core that is unstable. To avoid this happening, people responsible for the success of the business, being top management, must passionately lead OI themselves.

Corporate-wide OIs must be led by the person holding the most senior position in a company because the value-chain of an organization covers the whole spectrum of its business and is fully integrated into cross-department / functionality of modern systems. Elon Musk does this incredibly well.

Organizational Leaders often contemplate appointing a program-manager or less-senior manager to be in charge of corporate-wide OI. The best situations are when ultimate accountability for this type of OI, is the person at the top. Can you imagine Steve Jobs or Elon Musk assigning corporate-wide OI responsibility to someone else? No, they get it done themselves and that's partly why they've been so successful in achieving their respective missions.

The field of Organizational Change Management has failed at many things, the biggest mistake being, creating the impression that hiring a Change Lead consultant is going to 'make' the problem go-away.

Let's not make the same mistake with OI Leadership.

Whilst the use of people with an intimate knowledge of *coaching* organizations through Change **is** encouraged, the organizational leader might familiarize themselves with the pitfalls of handing over ownership of OI, to someone else.

To conclude, senior executives might consider for the sake of their career, to take active responsibility for the implementation of OI. In the case of a technology OI, they may not understand the technology, but for sure they understand about making improvements. Career advancements of senior executives may happen more frequently, if they always knew how much progress their divisions are making using OI and data about growth, as a result of successful OIs. Executives who do not achieve a specified strategic goal may be held accountable for their failure. It would be a pity if an OI could have helped, but it was never considered as a way to achieve success.

Executives may also come to understand that if an OI fails, there may be irreparable (at worst) or costly repercussions (at best). This is why an OI Practice is critical in assisting to implement OI, through OI Coaches and the OI Platform. For the same reason the finance department is there, they spend very little money themselves, but are accountable for ensuring liquidity and controls.

Read more about the OI Platform at OIActive.com.

23

THE ROLE OF LEADERSHIP IN INNOVATION

Leadership of an organization oriented towards positive social contribution and attractive shareholder value is not about greed, power, domination or any other narcissistic self-serving agenda. Genuine leadership is primarily how a person is experienced by others, in a way that fosters care and growth (Schuitema). Substantial research and common sense says that if a person is experienced as being sincerely caring and grows the people around them, that person will gain legitimate leader power. Their intent must, of course, be consistent and genuine.

In psychology there are numerous communication and attitude models, mostly they share the same principle that the listener, consciously or sub-consciously, attempts to ascertain the intent of the communicator.

In a typical work situation where the manager is not a legitimate leader (i.e.: there is no sincere care or real interest in the growth of the subordinate) the subordinate will generally believe that the communication coming from the manager is based on an objective to meet the demands of a more senior manager. Herein lies the difference between management and leadership, a subordinate following an instruction, or going about their job under the manager, will do as little as is required to stop from getting fired, or expressly disliked. It's easy to understand that this is not an environment in which innovation, a force of creative problem-solving, is going to thrive.

However we are in serious short supply of legitimate leadership in business, organizations and non-profits.

A subordinate who works under a legitimate leader will conduct their affairs with diligence and a proper, willing attitude because that is what the leader expects. It's easy to understand that this is the right environment in which to foster creative problem solving and thus innovation.

Thus leadership is important for innovation as well as other organizational aspects such as compliance, ethics and the risk of for example conflicts of interest.

The key difference between a manager and a leader is that the intent is quite different. A manager's intent is to keep their job and achieve planned objectives whereas the leader's intent is to care for their people, build competencies, and by facilitating the subordinate's growth, transcending mindsets thus being able to transition the company into a community that is focused on the same objective - innovation.

Attempting to change an organization expecting innovation and mind shifts without sufficient *legitimate* leadership, could be heading for trouble. Innovation generally requires larger effort and commitment than day-to-day operations and thus legitimate leadership is a real consideration in order to be successful.

What people need most during times of problem-solving and change, are leaders who sincerely care about them, whose words are trusted and are transparent, and provide 'whole truths' about the reasons for, and the objectives of, the change.

People will use their inner soul-energy when they are sincerely being looked after within a clear innovation framework. As discussed above, a potential OI risk is that the OI Leader is not experienced as a legitimate leader, but rather as a manager - resulting in less than favorable commitment and support of OI. Another risk related to leadership of OI can be when leadership of a corporate-wide OI, is delegated to someone other than the top executive.

In this case, the organization will always be sensitive to potential mis-alignment between the OI Lead and the top executive. If the two have a strained relationship, it is likely that, through the OI transition, there will be a wavering of the employee's loyalty (depending on the tide of pain and gain that the OI brings). If an organization wants to effect a corporate-wide OI, the top executive must lead the OI with a firm hand, having an equal but fair regard for the OI objectives and the needs of the stakeholders.

OI pains will be experienced, but the leader must remain vigilant to the objectives whilst caring for stakeholders and inspiring them to grow through the OI - a key reason why the business case is so important.

The leader must, intelligently, stand firm in his/her decisions, bearing in mind that their credibility as a leader is ultimately based on the quality of the business case. In other words, whenever an OI Leader makes a statement to the effect: "We are doing this *because...*" the statement must be believable and, for good governance sake, *be* true. The business case for an OI is expected to provide an honest, no-nonsense, comprehensible and logical framework of strategic drivers.

What many business leaders do is promise paradise to their employees – perhaps a world-class IT system - positioned as the answer to all the problems, or new ways of doing business that will result in a better life for all.

How many business leaders have said "We have to Change so that things can stay the same"? Change is the way life works, it is how survival happens. Survival cannot happen without innovation and this is more so in today's times than ever before. More and more people are starting to understand that change is as necessary as eating – and in that sense we can look to 'eat-up' OI opportunities. There is a principle in social evolution that is quite similar to organizational evolution, and that is, the more people are 'squashed' in terms of freedom of speech and ideas, the stodgier the people become. Stodgy organizations are the bureaucratic/government type, too scared to voice opinions, too complacent to take action and who follow instructions to the book - as long as someone is watching. Stodgy organizations are sometimes the least-complex to change because employees are sure no-one is going to get fired, so they just sit back and wait for the new-assignment letter or early retirement offer. But, they lack the energy that change often requires to really give the new way of doing things the boost it needs.

People in stodgy organizations believe that someone else is responsible for OI, and that someone is going to do the right thing - sometime. So... employees will just wait for new instructions.

An automotive manufacturer that re-structured its business resulted in two-engineers not having any work to do. For twelve years all they did was a bare minimum - play computer card games and eat at the canteen.

The role of leaders in OI is to inspire and motivate people so that the soul-energy of the organization is alive and responsive to the requirements of, not only a once-off change, but continuous, positive innovation.

Stodgy managers will result in very little innovation. Make the call, put people who are hungry for innovation in management positions and observe how, within the Coaching OI approach, they can make an organization truly innovative.

24

SOUL ENERGY

Understanding some of the key differences between effective and ineffective OI requires a basic appreciation of the link between the human psyche (soul) and innovation.

It is fast becoming fact that companies who "de-humanize" their people, and relegate them to mere "human resources" are not going to be perceived as positive contributors to society and are less likely to survive. Further, it is becoming apparent that a more 'spiritual' or 'soulful' view of people is required in order to adequately attract and keep the best talent. Some like to refer to the 'soft' side as the 'soul' side.

It is recognized that people are more energized being treated as 'souls' rather than 'human resources'. In this sense, 'psyche'-'ology' (study of the soul) can offer real value.

Accepting this soul principle is the first step towards understanding and effecting real OI. Management are responsible for their subordinate's souls, (some might say 'well-being') in the workplace **and** the experience that stakeholder's souls have in their dealings with the organization. OI Needs the creative energy of good souls, therefore souls need to be managed with the right intent, don't be an a**hole. You can get the best out of people without being an a**hole. An instructed or intimidated soul does little to innovate. Rather, an inspired soul, given the opportunity to unleash his or her potential in a problem situation, is just the kind of "We can do this..." soul you need for innovations that really need creative and committed energy from their people. This is where *real* psyche-ologists can help.

OI Is the key to unleashing your company's potential 'soul' energy – a very exciting thought indeed. The promise of transcendence and transition to a new desired state is a great motivator, if the intent is true and transparent.

Through the process of OI, it is often an eye-opening experience witnessing the people who become OI Innovators. Finance people, maintenance people, security people, workshop people, debtors' clerks – you may be surprised at the amount of 'soul-energy' available, just waiting for an opportunity to become an OI Innovator (About 7-15% of employees). We are not all born of equal logical, intellect, or academic aptitude, but we are all born with the potential to innovate.

>>> ***OI is not a full-time job,***
it's a full-time attitude.

There's a saying "Some people **make** things happen, others **watch** things happen and the rest **wonder** what happened." Which third, do you think, is going to thrive in the future?

The more people making strategic OI happen - the more successful your organization's strategic performance can be. Kaplan and Norton wrote excellent books on how to achieve strategy-focused organizations. They emphasize that one of the key building blocks that must be in place to achieve a 'strategy-focused' organization, is that all employees be part of strategic dialogue. However, top management generally isolate themselves for two days a year or every quarter, drafting strategic objectives and plans, using top management terminology, and then expect the rest of the organization to buy into and achieve the strategic objectives without them being a part of the process. In order to achieve a 'strategy-focused' organizational community, people must be brought into the strategic process – their 'souls' aligned to the organization's goals, starting with mission and vision. This can only be achieved through a well-intentioned, properly structured strategy and *team* performance framework.

Whilst the 'soul' side of OI is exciting discussion for some, for others it may be too 'fuzzy'. At this point a certain nonnegotiable statement needs to be internalized by anyone wanting to create a more OI Active organization:

>>> *'To succeed in OI, empathy is absolutely required, to understand what employees need at the deepest level.'*

For many, this concept may seem alien and some will disregard this statement completely. Certainly, many organizations who are only focused on the bottom-line, do quite well without any regard for their employees whatsoever, consider the success of unethical sweat-shops. Nevertheless, as organizations face pressures in a world where there is an ever increasing demand to focus on and report non-financial aspects, and where certain human-related factors are becoming more and more important (think diversity), business cannot stop and must continually improve the way they do business. John Elkington's 'Triple Bottom Line Reporting' (TBL), is evidence of a global shift to social and environmental responsibility and sustainability (TBL is 27 years old, and has just been updated). How does an organization get this right? How can employees be aligned to the objectives of, for example, TBL goals and also become a part of the OI process?

Another practical reason for understanding people's feelings is that they can be 'signals' that help us manage certain risks and issues. If we are in touch with the feelings of employees, then we have the ability to build risk profiles and 'manage' the risks that are clear risk signals. Therefore, being able to understand how feelings often become a destructive force in an organization, is key to managing risk to OI. Naturally, where feelings are being expressed, there must be an environment of credibility. OI Coaches and Innovators who are not trusted or who are nonchalant towards people's feelings will never hear 'the truth' until it is too late. Taking into consideration the management theory of employees balancing the scale of fairness, ignoring feelings will be met with a lack of commitment. For centuries, it was widely accepted that people had to work in order to get paid. That no longer holds true as people can now surf the net, socialize on multiple platforms, take breaks the entire day in the office, and still get paid. Even better, remote workers can do whatever they want, so long as they're achieving goals, and still get paid. People are attracted to doing their best, so long as they want to. Other the bare minimum, is what they'll give. In trying to understand the processes for OI, one must try and understand people's feelings and perceptions as the foundation of successful innovations and agility to implement innovations. No matter who you are, anybody looking at their own emotional intelligence, spiritual intelligence (understanding the connectedness between ourselves and others, and our world), and acknowledging shortfalls, can begin the process of growth and may enjoy the new experiences it can bring. One may even - through this process - begin understanding one's own soul. Maslow's little-known later-work, explains in his second version of the Hierarchy of Needs, that the capstone of a person's life is 'Self-transcendence'. This is where true psychology can be understood.

Hence the saying, 'to change the world, we must start with ourselves'. Wouldn't it be great if we taught that hierarchy of needs at management school?

25

THE ROLE OF MANAGERS

The history of modern management varies – consider a New Lanark factory (Scotland), owned by a forward-thinking industrialist, Robert Owens. He gave employees comfortable housing, training opportunities and offered an open-door policy access to management. This may seem a typical modern company, but considering that these practices at New Lanark started in the late 1800's it would seem in stark contrast to what is generally understood about the industrial revolution. From Owen's approach to the American concept of Scientific Management and the European concept of Classical Management, they all aimed to achieve the same thing, which was using people to achieve shareholder wealth. However, classical management (which was founded on works by the likes of sociologist Max Weber) placed people into organized systems just like cogs, they were not considered people, rather functions. In contrast, the American scientific school worked with studies and statistics which led to the realization that if workers were treated well, they worked better. This American scientific principle was accepted by both management and workers, because workers were able to be more people-like in their place of work as opposed to Europe's 'cog in the machine view'. Charlie Chaplin's black and white movie skit titled 'Modern Times' depicts the Classical School very well. However, both schools adopted the view that people were to be controlled and influenced in any manner that would achieve greater returns.

The Human Relations view, however, brought to the forefront the reality that most people work best when they are within social frameworks that we might call today, corporate communities, which, when based on the right set of corporate values, can be trusted to do their best. Within these varying management views one common aspect remained a challenge. This was to find ways to reduce the psychological and productivity impacts as a result of Organizational Change, and so Organizational Change Management interventions and programs became the default approach for doing this.

The Human Relations view being the most prevalent in the U.S. for example, requires a different approach than organizations that use classical view management theories.

Leading a human-centric organization through change,

requires that the leaders of the change be sincere, credible and have a deep, genuine passion for caring and growing people. These business leaders must connect with the working community and gather the trust of the formal and informal leaders within the organization. Transparency and mutual respect, equal to equal, must become the ultimate objective between OI Leaders and the formal and informal leaders. This is the only way to start the leadership of OI in a human-centric organization, or one that wants to become more human-centric.

When leading OI in the 'Classical Management' organizations, the approach that works best is good old fashioned honesty and direct engagement leadership. Don't waste time on seeking buy-in just go directly to the plan, be prepared and get the job done.

Educated individuals of any cultural background will be supportive of the business case through their understanding of business and economics etc., whereas lesser educated people will stick together and group-think their way through, latching onto words of the informal leaders - whether they echo the message of management or not is always a risk. This is one of the reasons for adequately educating the workforce because there are very real dangers to productivity in group-think scenarios amongst uneducated people.

Consider that if an uneducated or unconvinced leader argues against a specific OI, the community will follow the leader without really understanding the dynamics and reasons for the change, evermore the case for developing informal leaders, into well-educated, well-meaning OI Coaches.

Generally around the world, characteristics of managing change are the same. Kurt Lewin, gave the Organizational Change Management process three phases: (1) the known present, (2) the transition and (3) the desired outcome. His view was that the transition phase was the most painful and unless it was well-planned and well-executed the desired outcome would not be realized.

A lot of money has gone into technological innovations, but not much has gone into developing managers into real OI Coaches, it's time this changed, now that there's strong examples, and business cases to do so. Business leaders, typically, don't know how to improve collaborative cross-functional systems, processes and people, OI Coaches can help with that.

Education and understanding of how enterprise architecture, *specifically Service Oriented Architecture* works and how OI Processes stabilize the organization whilst bringing the OI to life, is critical, to ensure that the transition phase is *less painful and the outcome more successful.*

In most countries, improving the way the business works has been delegated over the decades to managers who have 'soft-skills' and are likely responsible for training employees, fitting within HR. One of the big challenges that HR departments have had, is the increasing focus of, for example the diversity agenda. Developing adequate improvement processes have NOT been their key-focus over the last two decades. However, this has not stopped the increasing responsibility for improving the respective organization being incorrectly dumped at their door. Because HR, typically, does not have a realistic budget for improving the organization, and does not have the chance to share responsibility, so the notion of OI delegating OI to HR, would fail before it has begun. OI Needs to be a CEO 'thing'.

As a solution, the HR department could make recommendations to executive management related to training and developing OI Coaches. If they put this to the executives, then OI has a real chance of being implemented. Next, and because OI is often required to achieve strategic objectives, an OI Policy can be introduced (More about this later.) And of course as part of recommending an OI Strategy, HR can propose an OI Platform to assist the OI Coaches. The whole package is a no-brainer. Strategic Coaching OI by executives, from an executive level can help encourage Coaching OI becoming a daily function of all people in management and leadership positions. A question may arise, 'But what about the daily operational activities we need to attend to, as management?'. This is a clear sign of short-terminism propagated by unbalanced performance measures. The daily activities are undertaken by subordinates as management is supposed to strategize, lead, transform and coach, and as such they should very rarely be 'doing' daily activities, this is more of a supervisor's role. However, the mistake is often made of transitioning good technical or operational people into management, whilst forgetting about also transforming them into good managers and leaders. Most companies that went through change *were* in fire-fighting mode before the change and became even more so when going through, and after the change. Managers who don't grasp the full meaning of management principles, such as strategizing, leading, transforming and coaching, believe that they have been made managers in order to 'BOSS' people who were probably once their peers. For the wrong people, this is a 'total power-trip'. Computer systems can now be pre-configured to make decisions that may have been previously manual management decisions. Through system workflow, physical sign-offs, which used to take weeks, can now take seconds.

Some Information Technology systems can remove entire management levels of decision-making. There could be less technical people being made managers, and more technical people improving the output of organizations. Managers need to understand cross-functional processes, cross-functional systems and how to lead at a minimum, in order to become a successful manager in modern organizations.

Management might do well to consider the Liberal Art side of leadership, such as, caring for employees, supporting employee's needs and being and coaching OI to improve the team's strategic performance. Modern management have social and environmental responsibilities, and are expected to lead with a vision to become a sustainably growing organization making a positive contribution to society. Management positions are likely to set people up for failure if they are seen as a promotion from a technical position. Good technical people are more effectively retained when adequately rewarded, more so perhaps, than being given management positions. Organizations around the world desperately need good managers who can work effectively with technical people, to take advantage of the growth opportunities of the new economies that the fourth industrial revolution is bringing.

>>> *Managers, in coaching OI, will leverage 4IR*

25

OI AND CORPORATE CULTURE

Just as systems are altered within the parameters of the existing system infrastructure, so too, is OI done within the existing cultural 'structure' of the respective organization. This will likely involve having to change the culture, a whole upgrade in fact.

Understanding the organization's culture at the time of introducing OI to the organization, is critical to learning the organizational dynamics that can be used to assist with implementing OI Policy and building OI Capabilities. It is equally important to understand the potential corporate-wide risk that could be lurking just beneath the day-to-day apparent operational, employee stability. Unions are a key stakeholder in some organizations and can plan to use OI as a lever for negotiation. As such, unionized cultures must be addressed with this in mind. Obviously, it is better to approach implementing OI with the right community intent and evolve potential barriers into enablers of change.

Unions generally work well when they are sincerely

welcomed as key stakeholders in implementing OI Concepts. In return, unions would do well, to not use opportunities to participate in OI as levers for (for example) wage negotiations.

In all respects, the liberal arts side of management, caring for people, is part of the job of both unions and management. It is imperative in implementing OI, that trust remain intact with all stakeholder groups and key stakeholders. To effectively use organizational culture as an enabler, there are three constructs an OI Lead would do well to gather information on, and incorporate into the OI process data:

Leaders:

Who are the official and un-official leaders? Official leaders are those who are in power positions because of their job description and un-official leaders are leaders of the people. Occasionally they are the same person.

These people need to be identified as important stakeholders, the more influence they have, the more they can get involved with OI.

People in positions of power, can become legitimate leaders too and become great OI Coaches. This is the objective of the OI Practice Lead.

Stories:

Find the stories that 'go-around' the official and un-official channels, as these can be useful in understanding things that have happened that have had an impact on the organization's culture and people's psyche.

This is a good time for some 'psyche'-ology, understanding *which* organizational stories have had *what* effects on people's psyche and what stories could create positive effects on people's psyche. An example could be a previous change that had a really bad outcome and as a result left a negative perception as to the credibility of management with regard to managing change. There's also a treasure trove of stories in the organization's newsletter archives and company press-releases that can provide key information points that have fostered positive sentiment in the organization and can be threaded into OI communications.

Rituals:

Celebratory lunches, charity golf-days and monthly management forums are all examples of 'rituals' that can be used to assist the change. Building on a framework of rituals and using them to promote consistent change messages, both in word and deed, are important in obtaining support and ultimately organizational ownership of the OI processes.

OI Leaders can work out how to use these three culture-building constructs to develop a culture more focussed on successful OI.

26

OI AND CORPORATE GOVERNANCE

Because of fraud disasters like Enron and WorldCom, the United States implemented a governance framework known as Sarbanes-Oxley (SoX). The foundation of this framework is based on penalizing non-compliance – 'comply or else'. Unfortunately, many will say, it did not achieve the desired results. Other countries previously applied a similar approach however, with the principle of 'comply or explain' so where there is non-compliance, a reasonable explanation must be provided. For the most part, at a minimum, publicly listed companies around the world need to have some or other risk management processes in place, which govern amongst other things, compliance risk.

Business risk as a result of business projects can be substantial, look at HP for example, an old but well-known story where the implementation of a new system caused serious order backlogs and lost revenue. Having OI Processes and Systems in place is simply good governance as risk-response plans for responding to needs and going through the transformations required to these implement OIs. Surely for a company to fly the flag of good corporate governance, it must have proper OI Governance and Processes in place for OI?. In order for organizations to prioritize the implementation of OI Processes, good governance and in some countries compliance, can serve the agenda and safeguard against short-terminism and other risks.

27

THE OI SCHEDULE

In any organization there can be, at any one time, a number of OIs occurring. Very often these OIs occur in silos and they do not feature on the radar of top management, however, they are still successful but there can be a scenario where the result of the smaller OI can hamper the bigger OI and the other way around, where big OIs can totally overrun the smaller OI. In both instances, the smaller OI may have to wait its turn.

OI Prioritization

It is important that all OIs occurring in an organization be registered on an OI Schedule, similar to a project portfolio. This can be done well using the OI Platform. If this is properly managed then the impacted stakeholders are able to better understand the importance and priority of the OI requirements and its associated actions and impacts. It often happens, when there are multiple OIs occurring, that employees are unsure how to prioritize activities. An OI Schedule on the OI Platform with an indication of how change activities are to be prioritized will greatly support employee's prioritization requirements.

The OI Schedule is Serious Business

Taking OI seriously can help give it the priority it needs. There is so much energy put into solutions meant to solve problems, and even more energy and investment required to transform that solution into reality. Just ask Elon Musk, who might agree that in such processes, any wasted or misdirected energy is a most unfortunate situation. A wise OI Policy would be for senior management to be seen as 'OI Quality Gate Controllers' in the OI Processes to assess TRANSFORM and SCALE impacts on the organization. Where any required OIs and planned Business Actions are assessed will put the organizational operating core at risk, then that risk as to be managed. For example, identifying which stakeholders are going to be impacted and what the effect will be on those stakeholders, of all the OIs, at the same time, will highlight the question of practicality, of too much happening at the same time, resulting in confusion and panic.

Strategic objectives that are used in the OI Design Feasibility Study, are key in terms of prioritizing OIs. Stephen Covey's Time Quadrant can assist in understanding how to arrange the conflicting priorities. It will assist in determining that which is important vs. that which is urgent.

In the assessment of prioritizing OI, it's good practice to involve key stakeholders so that there are strategic discussions amongst more than just senior management of the organization. This consultative process is, in itself, a way to build a strategically-focused organization.

Consider using this opportunity to coach OI, assisting executives understand the reasons for the OI and in turn this will foster strategic conversations amongst the executive ranks, the value of which might be more impacts identified, that may need to be considered and attached to the OI TRANSFORM or SCALE data records.

Accountability

True leaders will take accountability for their organization and this means also taking accountability for strategic direction and achievement. The CEO of Time Warner only recently publicly apologized for the AOL acquisition, which has been labelled 'the worst deal of the century'. One has to ask that if he had involved all stakeholders in the business case... would he have gone through with it?

Once the strategic objectives are understood and stakeholders buy into these objectives, it becomes easier for OI Business Actions to be understood and implemented, because people understand *why* changes have to happen, this then serves as the guiding mission and vision (purpose and game plan).

28

OI PRINCIPLES

Transformation of the organization as a response to a new OI is really the bulk of the work in OI and involves many people. At the highest level it is simple to break down the management of TRANSFORMATION into two strategies, Transcendence and Transition. Transformation can only be achieved when these two strategies work off each other's processes to deliver real mindset and real-world changes.

Transcendence Strategy

Transcendence refers to the elevated mind-shift with regard to values, culture, leadership etc., of the organization about to go through an OI release, like a new office ordering office equipment for example. Maybe part of the mind-shift in the new office is going paperless, so the team would not be ordering printers.

  Some levers for transcendental change are found within the constructs of the corporate culture. Referring to the earlier chapter on culture and change, one can consider the use of the three constructs of organizational culture in achieving transcendence, (1) Leadership, (2) Stories and (3) Rituals. Organizational Development experts are great in developing and executing strategies aimed to create mind-shifts, transcending how things are understood as part of an organization's OI journey.

Transition Strategy

Transition refers to the business processes, policies, standard operating procedures, job roles etc. of that particular organization, and with the fourth industrial revolution upon us, some very interesting opportunities are around for example, intelligent robotic process automation which will create massive transitions in business, but sadly and unavoidably, put many out of work.

Transition requires the detailed analysis and management of all the impacted tangibles and intangibles in an organization, digital systems, processes, performance objectives, job descriptions etc. This is driven in some ways by business risk response plans, which result in actions created to prepare for the go-live of the OI, thus completing the Business Actions required for an OI TRANSFORM step.

OI Requires Transformation.

Transformation = Transcendence + Transition

Integrating Transcendence and Transition

In order to successfully combine these transformation processes of transcendence and transition, they must be synergistically integrated during the OI TRANSFORM 'Business Action'. They work together. All OI Transition activities, if executed from the OI Value Chain TRANSFORM process, 'working' the desired transcendence values into the activities whilst giving people reasons (performance objectives) for doing things in a well-communicated strategic context. All transcendence and transition activities when done in the context of an OI, will get a clear link from the OI Record, to the Corporate Strategic Objective Framework. The team mentioned previously, as an example, moving into nice modern offices, will be told that, as part of going paperless, no printers will be installed in the office, instead nice big display monitors will be provided. There's the transcended value and action being demonstrated in conjunction with each other.

The OI Leader can create more effective workstreams, by not allowing transition activities to be executed in the manner of old-style leadership or old-style values. Introduce the new, with the familiar by upskilling employees with OI Innovation and Coaching practices, instead of command and control leadership of the old, which creates a barrier to creativity, thus blocking OI.

OI Transformations requiring only the transition facility of transformation is relatively easy as this might only require the support of people who are more technically competent in terms of job design, process design etc. Going back to our example of a team in a new office, if they were a paperless office previously, then there's no need to focus on transcending the mindset away from using paper. It's imply a transition from one office to another. However, OI requiring only transition happens less often than OIs requiring a mind-shift change.

Change requiring a transcendent process can be more of a challenge, combining transcendence and transition strategies to achieve transformation. The transformation of management into leaders, or the transformation of mediocre or stodgy corporate values into values that endeavor to build an organization contributing positively to society, requires, in many cases, huge personal introspection and growth on the part of both leaders and the teams vested in supporting them. For many individuals, this is such an impossible process that they can't find it within themselves to commit to the objectives and associated activities, and end up resigning or being replaced before the transformation process is complete, thus missing out on the personal growth one gets during transformation, the very thing they need, in order to succeed in modern business.

Emerging markets as individual countries, have gone through incredible transformation in their fledgling years as new democracies and innovations focused on GDP growth. However, the transition process from old to new generally, has been very weak leaving the country vulnerable to corruption and open to people with wayward and devious politicized and/or self-serving agendas. It is also an opportunity for the youth of the country to step up to the challenge of driving economic reform with innovation. This is quite common in emerging markets.

Any transformation, coupled with well-planned and exquisitely executed transcendence and transition in order for the transformation to be sustainable, has a better chance of sustainable success. One could say that the transcendence is the mission (purpose) and transition is the vision (game-plan) for the transformed organization/country to become successful. Silicon Valley is a great example of where this is happening all the time. Youngsters come here to fill the gap, where thinking has not evolved, so transition-debt hangs, waiting for somebody to make it happen and be rewarded.

OI Principles

Having touched on the importance of the transcendence strategy as being the enabler of the transition strategy, the foundation principles of successful OI capabilities now has some context and can be introduced. If you're taking this book seriously and want to implement OI in your organization, start thinking about training your managers on these principles and including them in their performance indicators, to become OI Coaches. The 5 OI Principles are:

1. Coach OI,
2. Success Journeys,
3. DESIGN,
4. TRANSFORM,
5. SCALE.

The following chapters describe each principle and are important for OI Coaches to help employees understand, they can change the world, or at least the organization they work in, and the OI Value Chain is the way to do it.

29

PRINCIPLE 1: COACH OI

Responsibility for coaching OI in an organization could better leveraged if it is 'owned', by for example, the organization's OI Practice. It is also vitally important that senior management decide on the mission (purpose) and vision (game-plan) for their organization's Coaching OI, Capabilities and Processes that will require the allocation of resources, as detailed in an OI Policy.

Coaching OI as a Franchise

Thinking of Coaching OI as a franchise is a useful metaphor for helping people to understand what ownership of Coaching OI actually means. Ideally, the OI Practice sets up the OI Platform for the organization which will be there to enable the OI Processes across the organization, which are then 'franchised' out to OI Coaches (managers), where, in turn, those Coaches 'sell' the OI franchise services to their teams and stakeholders, then becoming an OI Platform and

Process provider for their department and stakeholders, increasing the efficiency of OI and reducing risks of negative disruption, because everybody is literally on the same page.

An organization can 'franchise' their OI Capabilities to the multi-stakeholder eco-system that organizations are the center of, for example in their supply-chain, or even to customers trying solve problems, themselves. Through an OI Policy, senior management of an organization make a commitment to support and enable processes for departments to Coach OI and empower department managers as OI Coaches to lead OI within that department, as franchise owners, ultimately accountable for successful OI. This 'OI Franchise' metaphor can help emphasize OI Ownership by all management, which in turn can build the right culture through the OI Value Chain and the respective multi-stakeholder eco-system.

It is vitally important that they own the OI Processes required for continued organizational success, as OI Coaches, working with the OI Practice – as they may be held accountable by shareholders and other stakeholders if the organization does *not* achieve its goals. Nobody below senior management will have the authority or strategic overview required to make the right decisions and drive collaboration of key stakeholders in situations where stakeholders are at odds with each other, which happens frequently in OI.

This is just one reason for the accountability of future success, to never be fully delegated. Top management must assume ownership of OI as a practice, throughout the organization.

The steps for getting senior management to own the OI Processes can be found in parts of this book explaining the TRANSFORMATION in the context of the OI Value Chain.

CoachOI.com also has great artifacts that can be used in this process of onboarding executive managers into OI Leadership positions.

30

PRINCIPLE 2: SUCCESS JOURNEYS

We covered aspects of Success Journeys earlier in this book, and this chapter extends the Success Journey conversation more to how we manage stakeholder groups we work with, when doing Success Journeys, and how we use the OI Platform at OIActive.com to do this.

An OI Platform is a set of databases that is a repository for data related to OIs, as a 'System of Records'. It enables collaboration, process, governance, work-flows, reporting, compliance and risk management where stakeholder groups are involved.

The first step in the OI Value Chain, DESIGN, requires identifying stakeholder groups we can then work with and use the Success Journey approach, identifying their mission, vision, strategies and associated strategic objectives, co-exploring challenges they may be having. Needs then surface related to what could them overcome their challenges.

The OI Platform is used to gather all this data collected from stakeholder groups. In business projects, the question of who is being impacted, even in the best of cases, is generally given a very rudimentary assessment and often stakeholder groups are 'forgotten' and key stakeholders left out of the process.

Case in point: *After conducting a corporate-wide climate survey at a large retail chain, we were invited to present the findings to the CEO. We were asked a very fundamental question "Did you include the central distribution centers?" It was a very defining moment in our presentation of the results, simply because our answer was "No" – what went through our minds was "How is this going to affect our presentation and our relationship with the client going forward?", also, "How the heck did we miss this?".*

His response was conspicuously neutral, although there was obviously a key lesson in it for us, and now for you – and that is, a prudent analysis of everyone being impacted by the OI inside and outside the organization must be done along with a high-level check on where stakeholder groups are going to require the most attention and support.

This analysis can be an assessment of:

- **Organizational Scope** - Specific definition of the organization's structure.
- **Internal Direct** – E.g.: A department or group of employees whose jobs are going to change.
- **Internal Indirect** – E.g.: Unaffected employee groups whose jobs are not going to change, but can be updated about the OI for general awareness and interest sake.
- **External Direct** - E.g.: Customers or vendors.
- **External Indirect** - E.g.: Industry interest groups.

At this level of stakeholder analysis only the stakeholder group is identified e.g.: Internal customers or external customers. The details of *individuals*, within the stakeholder groups will be obtained later in the process.

In the OI Platform, in these OI processes, there is a stakeholder analysis process where a database of these stakeholder groups are maintained in a system against categories like the ones above. In doing a stakeholder analysis, an organization can then use this database as a source of communications, using contact details like e-mail addresses for push communications such as flash news items by e-mail or messages from the CEO.

Once this level of stakeholder analysis (i.e. Stakeholder Groups) has been completed and **signed-off** by the respective management, the next activity can then begin.

At this next step, the exercise of identifying **key-stakeholders** is done as part of using the OI Platform. These people will typically represent, or be a channel of, communications for a stakeholder group. For example, it may not be that the OI Team communicates directly with external customers as it may be best that the head of marketing take on this role, who, in-turn will recruit the assistance of account executives to carry out OI messaging activities, with impacted customers. Another example is in regard to government departments, it may be best that the corporate government liaison officer does the 'talking' to government clients and so would be identified as the 'Key Stakeholder' of government stakeholder groups. The OI Practice will help to manage the OI Platform, working with such key stakeholders and their respective OI Coaches across the organization. In all matters pertaining to stakeholder communication, people who are respected, willing and able to be the communication 'portal' to a stakeholder group are better positioned to be more effective than people that don't have that social position. Remember the Aesop fable? Get as many people doing OI activities as possible.

If the entire sales team can be recruited into assisting to cascade customer OI messaging, where the customer is impacted, for example invoicing changes, that would be first prize. Please note these examples are representing only the impact on the customer and government stakeholder groups. There are many, many more stakeholder groups. Adding stakeholder data to the OI Platform ensures that their information is seen and can be used in Scale Plans and other OI Value Chain activities where they may be impacted. Once the 'Key-Stakeholders' have been identified, the next step of obtaining detailed information about individual stakeholders begins.

Using the OI Platform

Using the OI Platform at OIActive.com means that OI can be managed extremely effectively and through integration with mail servers and other systems can enhance efficiencies in the OI Value Chain.

The data that is used will be more effective if it is thoroughly cleaned, removing all errors before connecting or uploading. This information is then linked to one (or more) of the stakeholder groups from the above activity. Similarly supplier and customer details are obtained and uploaded into the OI Platform. Wherever there is master-data or bulk information or records, which has the details of individuals or stakeholder organizations, this would be loaded into the OI Platform for communications throughout the OI process. This makes it easier to slice and dice the numbers into the various categories of stakeholder groups and required involvement for alignment to the new way of business. This is to understand the effort required and enable the organization to manage the stakeholder engagement process in a quantifiable manner.

Once all the possible data has been obtained and uploaded into the OI Platform, or otherwise documented (if you are not going to use the OI Platform), an analysis can begin on the influence the stakeholders could have on the OI and respective transformation of idea to reality, and the degree to which they need to be involved in mind-shift exercises all needs to be considered.

When Elon Musk built his Tesla factory in China, he had to onboard the Chinese officials to make it happen, and would likely not have been able to achieve that objective, if he hadn't.

There are a number of categories that can be applied here when conducting the analysis, here are some for you to consider:

Category 1: Stability:

Does this stakeholder *absolutely* require stability of service or product supply during the OI Value Chain processes and activation? For example, there may be a large customer who cannot accept a longer supply time as a result of the OI – no matter how temporary. Whereas a smaller client could potentially accept longer supply times because they are not so busy. Another stakeholder example that requires absolute stability could be a charity organization that depends on perhaps, the delivery of food from a distribution center where their service feeds people.

Category 2: OI Makers

After discussions with stakeholders, you may find it prudent to note those who are initially supportive of the OI and respective organizational changes and are willing to be 'understanding' of the organization's expected operational instability resulting in temporary poor service levels. Some customers may not care about building solid long-term relationships with the changing organization and will threaten changing suppliers if they are negatively affected by the OI.

Internal and External Customers who really believe in the concept of partnerships will commit to supporting the organization through the OI process as long as there is transparency from the changing organization and there is a commitment that it will do its best to make things right if there are any problems in the supply of goods and/or services. The stakeholders who are not supportive of the OI may require a carrot of sorts. For example, the promise to them that the change will achieve the implementation of modern innovations, resulting ultimately, in quicker turn-around times on services. In which case, it would be prudent to put such Key Performance Indicators on the Service Level Agreement reports reflecting the 'before and after' measures in order to prove to the customer that the OI objectives have been achieved.

Category 3: OI Breakers

This indicator will identify the stakeholders who will be affected in a net-negative way. This could be, for example, employees who would have to be re-located. It could be suppliers who will have to build new Electronic Data Interfaces (EDI) in order to continue integrating with the changing organization's IT systems. This is the 'Pain' side of transformation.

Category 4: OI Winners

These are stakeholders who are likely to benefit from the OI. Possibly, the finance department will be able to complete the month-end reports a lot quicker than previously. This gain-point can be used to leverage certain requirements of the finance department in, perhaps, client and supplier master-data 'cleaning'. This is the 'Gain' side of transformation.

Who will Pain and who will Gain? Manage them accordingly. These are just a few examples.

Critical to the OI process is acquiring the signature of the OI Lead finalizing information about stakeholder groups, key-stakeholder nominations and individuals within stakeholder groups. It can easily happen that verbally it is agreed that all stakeholders have been considered, and then later in the process, one can be held accountable for overlooking a particular stakeholder group. If there is a signed-off stakeholder analysis document, then this can be a useful baseline reference.

Innovation is a bit like a walk through a forest. The more data and information you have about the environment ahead, the better you can prepare. Don't get stuck in the 'paralysis by analysis' situation, avoid it if you can, and remain diligent to managing the environment, optimally using the OI processes, systems and data about the people being affected and data about those who can influence the OI.

31

PRINCIPLE 3: DESIGN

Continuous growth requires continuous injection of capital. Most of the time this means other people's money, which is never free and for regular businesses means competing in the market for capital. There is an accounting definition for the rate of interest charged for the use of capital in an organization known as the 'Internal Rate of Return' or 'IRR'. This is the interest rate that OI Owners need to incorporate into their feasibility when they calculate the return on the OI Investment. The optimal use of capital is a culture which Steve Jobs is well known for lamenting on, at Apple and in his lesser known business, NEXT Computers. Nickel-and-diming, as he put it, should be the way things get procured not only as an 'early days' startup, but also as a large organization.

The idea of formulating business cases is irksome to most managers, but a person who has been coached in OI, will see it as a way to test the ground-up demand for the OI and the true OI costs of the TRANSFORMATION and SCALE steps in the OI Value Chain.

Let's take a look at two business case perspectives, top-down and bottom-up used in OI DESIGN Feasibility studies, focused on financials.

Top-Down Feasibility

This part of the business case is based on high-level assumptions and arrives at figures using broad-based market numbers, whether the market is an internal stakeholder group or external real customer market segment.

Bottom-Up Feasibility

This part of the business case details the initial investment required in the OI, and the cost to transform the OI from idea to reality, whether that be a small OI, or the introduction of an electric vehicle to the mass market. It may be for internal or external customers and the operating capital to run it. It will also detail the unit economics where, for external customers it may be real currency value or for internal customers where the measure may be in savings.

Managing the business case with a calibrated top-down/

bottom-up view integrated with the execution processes ensures that the initial expectations of the OI are kept under control. OI Processes work well when they provide dynamic updates to the business case in its ROI measurement.

32

PRINCIPLE 4: TRANSFORM

Project Management principles are great for building an asset where it describes a sequence of tasks required to, for example, build a house, a physical thing. However, Project Management principles for Business Projects require a very different set of principles. Traditional Project Management assumes that for example, building a new house has no impact, however, making changes to the structure of a house has a lot of impacts. Oftentimes, Project Management principles are extended to include Organizational Change Management which is supposed to address business impacts. Often 'People Change Managers' are used to do this, but they don't have the understanding of how business works, to do this adequately. This results in project go-lives being a mass of confusion. The TRANSFORM step in the OI Value Chain solves these problems, replacing the need for Project and Organizational Change Management. Hopefully they would have been trained to become OI Coaches!

> **When actions and impacts are planned and executed as one, you're doing Transformation. Applying Transcendence and Transition strategies, means doing Transformation, more effectively.**

Transforming a business woks better with a balanced approach which includes not only the sequencing of actions, but also identifying the resulting impact and its respective risk response in order to ensure the action is successful. For example, breaking a wall down in a house requires an assessment on the load on top of that wall and the impact response is the action of inserting a support beam where the wall stands, before being knocked down!

This approach in OI also needs to integrate into the OI Value Chain, it is not a standalone 'ivory tower' where things are done in a 'black box'. More on this to follow.

33

PRINCIPLE 5: SCALE

Effective OI is about how to SCALE Up the OI *into* the organization, once launched. Often in the organizational context, benefits realization is used to measure and improve the business case ROI of projects, but does not always attempt to identify the readiness of the users or employees, nor plan tasks to improve OI buy-in and adoption by the stakeholder groups. Benefits are identified and realized as part of the SCALE step.

The Subject Matter Expert, or SME of a particular business process, for example accounts-receivable, is the person who re-engineers the 'to-be' desired state for their process and can make a great OI Innovator. There may be one SME for each key process or department. This person normally has seniority and experience on their side and has been given the authority to design the best way of doing business and continually innovates, in a consultative process with respective business stakeholders. This effectively becomes the primary (delegated) function of business analysts or process-engineers. What the SME could also be doing is facilitating impact workshops, whereby predictable impacts as a result of OI Value Chain TRANSFORMATION Business Actions, are registered in the respective Business Action record on the OI Platform, linked to key processes and the respective stakeholder groups impacted by changes in processes.

The next step is to prioritize the impact in terms of how it will affect which stakeholder groups and also understand the risk to the OI, if the impacted stakeholders may not have been fully prepared in time for the activation of the OI or the Business Actions. In order to prepare stakeholder groups for the OI, 1) Communications, 2) Education and 3) Training are key to ensuring OI value can deliver as planned. In the case of OI, SCALE Plans are planned and rolled-out into specified stakeholder groups. The identified impacts will need to be communicated by the OI SCALE Workstream member assigned ownership of an OI. Also, where the impact requires, an OI SCALE Workstream member needs to be assigned ownership to design education programs developed around stakeholder's learning about the OI, in order to be adequately enabled for the new way of doing business. The SCALE Team member may also need to 'cascade' training workshops for stakeholders to attend. In OI, training takes education programs a step closer to engaging with the new policy, capability, process or technology that may be part of the OI, to train where, for example, to click, to create a new sales order.

Regarding business alignment, a practical warehouse management OI scenario is the re-numbering of storage bins and locations in a warehouse because of a new app related OI, and standardization across the organization of storage locations. This is an impact that may require senior management leadership. The risk of this not being done by the 'go-live' date is that warehouse staff will not be able to find stock if the new system picking-slip has the new storage location numbers but the physical bins and locations still have the old numbers. This could potentially be highly disruptive on customer service and production where the material is required to feed a production line.

As to the number of impacts registered, it all depends on the complexity and disruption of the OI, also, the dynamics of the existing culture and the OI appetite of stakeholders.

It is always a good idea to use the OI Platform as part of the Business Action Impact activities – all the tools to do this properly will greatly improve the success of the OI Workstreams, which we will learn about in the next chapters.

Using the wisdom of the Aesop fable introduced earlier in this book, get as many people as possible participating in the OI Value Chain, the bigger the footprint of the OI Value Chain, the more effective the organization will be, both internal and in the market.

The process for registering OI Value Chain SCALE impacts is as follows:

Step 1:

Create awareness of the OI Practice, and their activities related to Coaching OI, amongst the stakeholder groups.

Step 2:

Hold further workshops with a balance of senior business people *and* the doers, i.e. people who actually do the job. Explain the vision for the OI in the context of the business problems it is attempting to solve, and then get input on how this new way might be achieved along with the associated impacts, where the organization will have to change, to incorporate the OI.

Step 3:

Once the new way is presented as a diagrammatical process, and in steps, to the same group of people, facilitate a session whereby people provide their insights as to what may have to be changed in order to do business the new way.

Register these impact ideas from the SME group and put this list of registered impacts on the OI Platform for all to see. If the internal stakeholders think of impacts that the SME group has not listed, then they could register impacts themselves. If the the OI Platform system is being used, then any stakeholder will have access to register an impact for the respective business analyst or SME to assess.

Through the process of registering the impacts in these workshops, provide some details as to which process this particular impact belongs, such as 'Accounts Receivable' or 'customer opportunity management' in the CRM environment. Also, whilst registering the impact, rank the importance of the impact with regard to how much damage will be caused to the organization if it is not ready in time - use the following categories:

Category: High – will directly disrupt external customer service. For example, telephonic ordering by customers – if the phone-number has changed this will certainly disrupt customer service and must be listed .

Category: Medium - will create internal bottlenecks, thereby disrupting customer service. For example, the accounts department credit-management process, if a customer is waiting at a counter and their credit-limit will not allow an urgent purchase, however, they have made payment of the account. The credit-controller will have to be quickly integrated into the situation to allow the customer to make a purchase. This can be done by lifting the credit-lock on that customer's account once the claimed deposit has been verified.

Category: Low – will not have material effect on processes, but must be done, for example, cancelling dot matrix printer paper orders if the new printers are to be A4 lasers.

Once the impetus of impact registering has begun then the process of assigning ownership to get business ready at an individual impact level must happen.

Each registered impact will be owned by someone. At this point in time, bring forward enthusiastic people committed to the OI. Ask them if they are willing to ensure that the business is prepared for the OI by educating people about a particular impact, and how they must do things differently in their respective roles for a change in process. If, for example, customer account numbers are going to change, then one person in accounts will own this change impact and ensure that through either communication and education workshops, or one-on-one sessions, that all impacted people and departments are aware of the fact that account numbers will be changing.

Have these people update their progress, for example, in the OI Platform where their alignment efforts can be tracked. If they have planned ten workshops to align ten groups of people to the new account numbers and they have completed six of them, that person would then be sixty percent complete. Build a flag into the impact register so that if there is something going terribly wrong, the owner of the impact can notify the Business Impact Management Team-lead immediately by clicking on the problem item's escalation indicator. Aim to complete the business readiness activities of the high category impacts at least 3 weeks before 'go-live'. Medium impacts are expected to be complete by 'go-live' and low-impacts can be completed within an agreed time-frame after the 'go-live' date.

The OI Platform provides online dashboards so that anybody approved for access, can see the progress of the OI Value Chain activities.

Education and Training

Education and Training in the OI is important for **enabling** people to be able to adequately carry out the responsibilities of the process roles that they have been given in the new way of doing business. In many cases of OI, there are new things that will have to be understood. It may be, for example, education about new purchasing policies and/or new system training.

Whatever the new requirement is of the employee, learning will be key to the employees 'adaption' to the new way of doing business. Collectively, the better the learning process for all, the quicker corporate performance can be stabilized and the objectives of the OI, realized.

Often, training executed within a tight budget is not enough to prepare people. For this reason it is important to look past the immediate perceived training requirement and understand that successful organization's endeavor to be learning organizations with OI Coaches. Peter Senge, one of the 'thought' leaders who has contributed substantially to the field of Organizational Development, emphasized the concept of learning organizations in his book 'The Fifth Discipline: The Art and Practice of the Learning Organization' (Senge, 1990).

This book was written at a time when it was becoming apparent that changes were happening in technology, logistics, supply-chain management etc., with such velocity that people were on a continual learning curve, oftentimes running to stand still.

So whilst the OI in question may have a learning requirement, the principle of a learning organization can be effective reinforced as part of OI if it doesn't already exist as an organizational goal.

What makes a learning organization really work is that cost-centers for training and education, infrastructure (computer training rooms for example), processes, resources and culture are *already* in place to put people through learning interventions. Most times in OI, all this has to be set up from scratch for the upcoming OI learning requirements, especially at the SME level. If it's not set up then there is a lot of work to do and a lot of money to be spent preparing rooms etc.

If the organization is not yet at the stage of being a learning organization, there will be a budget problem, management will generally attempt to squeeze the budget, resulting in incomplete or ineffective training, and corporate performance will suffer. Unless senior management agree with the principles of a learning organization and make money available for building the required infrastructures and processes for learning to happen, the desired state is unlikely to be realized. The education and training processes can be used, not only for the current OI requirements, but to achieve a learning organization environment that can remain in place long after the respective OI is complete.

The difference between *learning* and *training* is that *learning* is a continuous managed *process* whereas *training* is more a *specific* isolated event. For example, training may be 'how to do a journal entry in an accounting system', whereas a learning program will enable that accounting clerk to become a better accounting clerk.

One of the big failures of, for example, IT projects, is that system-training is completed without regard to the OI impacts that have happened in the business processes that the IT project is enabling. What typically happens is the end-user of a new system they've only been trained on, has some idea about what to 'click' in the new system, but doesn't have much knowledge about anything else in the new business processes. The new way of business using the terminology of how things are expected to be done, is more effective when started early in the project, system training comes later.

Educate early, train late.

At some point in a project, people will begin making statements about how important training is, so they start training too early without access to a training system and by the time the system goes live the end-users have forgotten what to do. Another very common situation is when the new system keeps getting modified before go-live and the innovations come so fast and furiously that the end-users can't keep up with learning all the new innovations. People then become fearful of their incompetence which in turn leads to all sorts of psychological problems - resulting in very poor readiness for the change.

Education about, for example, new procurement policies must start as soon as the new policies have been signed-off by senior management in the early stages of the business analysis, and the new way of doing business becomes accepted. To reiterate: ***Educate early, train late.***

If the changing organization has the luxury of computer training centers and people can be trained earlier, they would learn more effectively, when they can be trained on at least the basics, such as system navigation for example and have a demo environment to explore. As more of the system becomes finalized, then begin introducing these newly developed unit-functional system-components at training sessions. It is unlikely that full cross-functional processes can be trained until quite late in the project, as the last system development phase of a project is usually 'integration testing', where the processes that run through multiple departments and functional areas can be completed and the 'bugs' fixed. Only then can these complex processes be trained.

The SCALE Process to use while creating documentation for the OI Education and Training Management Process could be structured and signed-off in the sequence as follows:

The SCALE Charter

This document outlines requirements and principles that will be used as the basis for the SCALE process. The charter will also outline the governance structure i.e.: documents, steering-committees, important sign-off meetings, etc.

The SCALE Strategy

This document outlines the approach and detail of all items that will be required (venues, computers, trainers, documents etc.) with a high-level time framework, inclusive of forecasted costs.

The SCALE Plan

Who, when, where, what etc.

Learning Curriculums

The Courses and subsequent lessons that make up the courses: course to job, role mapping, and lesson objectives for example.

The Training Event Schedules

Detailed schedules including the following:

- Training event tracking code or serial number
- Course name
- Lesson name
- Roles associated with the training event
- Facilitator's details
- Venue details
- Training Document to be used
- Equipment to be used
- Preparation requirements
- Learners that need to attend

Evaluations

Learners evaluate facilitator, and, facilitator evaluates learners. This is used to assist with the quality of facilitation and identify who are consistently having problems in learning.

Reports

Reports of learner's competence and progress of the training.

The Templates – What templates are required e.g.: Training documents, meeting minutes, certificates etc.

The working document repository – Where is all this going to be kept? A central training server perhaps? An Intranet Learning Portal – a place where people can go for training material, training event dates etc.

Audit trail – Everything must be done in such a way as to be easily auditable. Training coordinators in all departments/sites to assist in the co-ordination of training events. In the OI Platform, the Education and Training system is embedded as part of the Enabling Process.

Part Four

Implementing OI

34

THE OI DESIRED STATE

The OI Value Chain needs to be be adequately managed using a robust framework that consists of planning, budgeting, resource-management, tasks, time-frames, progress-reporting and mitigation of risks and issues, for OI to be effective.

This might sound like a project, but it's not. The reason is that a project works in a 'Project Management Office' mindset, owning delivery. In OI, the departments own OI delivery. What is required for managing OI, are the application of the management functions (strategize, lead, transform and coach) within the OI Value Chain positioned around the core of the business, directly integrating with the core of the business. The OI Value Chain processes when positioned around the business core, can more easily integrate with the finance processes which run through every facet of the organization, ensuring robust and dynamic feasibility management.

Unfortunately many well-meaning and potentially valuable

OI initiatives are setup as projects, and launched but not managed as an integrated component of business as usual, leaving yet another potential world-changing OI, dead. The old adage 'what's worth doing, is worth doing well' is very applicable, especially when dealing with a situation where an organization, its shareholders and other stakeholder's livelihood, is at stake.

As we go through the remainder of this book, it would be worthwhile to try and understand how the principles of OI, as mentioned in the previous chapters, can be managed by every single line-manager and those handful of employees that seem to make everything happen. The natural innovators (7-15% of managers and employees) will want to own and execute the processes of OI in an organization, to bring that OI to reality, not a project management office, which is great if you're executing a civil engineering project, but terrible for enterprises and business ownership. The remainder of this book will provide guidelines and tips as to how this can be done.

More specifically, the next two chapters focus on the OI policies, charters and capabilities required to establish the foundations of the OI process, and how to build the OI Workstreams. These will be followed by two chapters that introduce two Key Objectives and their respective OI phases, for implementing OI, which is a practical guide on how to manage the OI processes with the application of specific principles and practices.

There's no surprise, that to implement OI in an organization, we suggest using the OI Value Chain.

With OI implemented, the organization can consider themselves to be 'OI Active'.

35

OI POLICIES AND CHARTERS

Abraham Lincoln said "Give me six hours to chop down a tree and I will spend the first four sharpening the axe.". The preparation required to implement the OI processes involves mostly the creation and documentation of OI concepts, alignment of approaches amongst the management levels and signed acceptance of certain governance processes and escalation guidelines. This is done using OI Governance Policies. Writing an OI policy is the collective effort of a number of like-minded people combining their shared values, concepts and ideas together for the purpose of presenting their formalized OI model, and proving their cohesion as a group, with a brand new mission to scale OI in the organization. This is very important as it will be the first discussions and commitments that a team of executives, and their respective management teams, will have. It is at this point that the 'flavor' of things to come, is going to start. Setting the 'flavor' is a big part of managing OI as this will be the foundation for the organization's OI strategy, moving forward. It is here that the messaging, values and personal objectives are shared. It is also at this point that the Principles of *Organizational Development* must be highlighted, and agreement reached that these principles be the guiding principles of OI in the organization. Some of these principles could be as follows:

- No spoon-feeding, let the natural tendencies surface as a result of initiative, also, it is important to encourage people to learn from the official communications and learning processes.
- Use the opportunity to build a learning organization.
- Adopt the Aesop principle of Change and entrust Change activities to as many people as possible.
- Focus on principles of leadership, reduce focus on immature management practices like micro-management.
- Develop strategies, manage performance and discourage continuous focus on urgent activities or knee-jerk activities hence becoming strategy-focused.
- Empower people to be driven by personal mastery, meaningful Change contribution and enablement of their organizational community.
- Encourage personal growth.
- Drive attention to detail.

The OI Policy is the backbone of all OI activities, it is not simply a document. Once the OI Charter is complete, an accompanying presentation that encompasses the key points of the OI Policy and charter will provide a useful summary of what the organization plans to do with OI. The executives of the company must be educated about what is in the policy and to be made sure that they understand their roles and responsibilities in the OI Processes.

The policies that needs to be developed, understood, and signed-off by the senior management who are involved, are:

1. *Coaching OI Policy:*

Focus on OI Ownership, leadership, capabilities and the approach to the OI processes and the management thereof.

2. *Success Journey Policy:*

Focus on the approach to identifying, analyzing and managing OI Stakeholders.

3. *DESIGN Policy:*

A policy will determine what amount of risk and investment return is required to accept feasibility outcome.

4. TRANSFORM Policy:

Focusing on how changes to the business are going to be managed in terms of analyzing the impacts of the new way of doing business and then aligning business aspects and people to the new way (change of stationery, new chart of accounts, new customer account numbers, new storage locations etc.).

5. SCALE Policy:

Focusing on the communication methods, channels and two-way communication process with stakeholders – this will unpack how perception risk is going to be identified and then mitigated within a proposed communications framework.

Focus on the approach to educating and training people on the new way of doing business – Think "Enabling". This would include a system key-user (super-user) or Subject Matter Expert development program.

It wild be useful to managers, if the policies flow from a **Corporate OI Strategy** so the policies will have sufficient detail in it to give the resulting strategies very clear objectives that can be copied across (literally) into new OI process documents (or uploaded into the OI Platform).

When this is complete, build in the detail activities, timeframes and OI Process roles clarification, using charters for each OI Workstream. It is good to keep terminology consistent throughout the communications, roles and documentation processes. For example, if the Policy describes a, OI Impact Survey tool, use only that naming convention, and not for example, Risk Analysis Survey whilst referring to the same thing. Try as much as possible to use the same terminology throughout all OI documentation, that way, people who are on the periphery of the OI can follow and understand the themes all the way through. The terminology in this book is mostly generic, and you are encouraged to use the OI Platform at OIActive.com and CoachOI.com coaching collaboration platform, which has OI Documentation templates for registered members.

As you can see, nearly all the 'Ownership' principle of OI, within the Preparation part of implementing OI processes, is focused on coaching leaders to understand the processes, accept responsibility of the OIs and required changes, commit to the process and learn how the process of personal continuous growth can be developed with OI. This education, understanding, and acceptance of leadership roles is done through developing the policies discussed above in conjunction with the respective leaders.

36

BUILDING OI CAPABILITIES

The OI Principle chapters were intended to introduce key principles that would need to be understood and supported across the organization, so that OIs can get the support they need from the people who will be affected, and/or will be using the OI. As with everything, timing is of the utmost importance. It is best if the OI Principles (as discussed in the previous chapters) are handled by different OI Workstreams, representing every department around the world, in the case of multi-national organizations. These OI Workstreams work together, and support the OI Value Chain for each OI depending on how the OI impacts stakeholder groups. They are are spread across the organization. The OI Coaches will educate all OI Innovators to enter OI Data onto the OI Plattorm so that the collaboration required to DESIGN, TRANSFORM, SCALE many different OIs simultaneously can be done effectively. It is a good idea to introduce the concept of the OI Workstreams in the OI Policy Charter as previously described. The people leading these streams will logically be the senior executives who have signed ownership of the OI Capabilities in the Coaching OI document, as discussed in the chapter "Principle One: Coaching OI". They in turn constitute and report into the (1) OI Leadership Team, that is led by the Chief Executive (or highest accessible executive).

When it comes to deciding which executive is best positioned to lead one of the three OI Workstream, here are a few suggestions:

- The DESIGN workstream can be led by one executive, as Success Journeys require stakeholder details in order to send and receive communications relating to Success Journeys etc. These two teams could be led by a marketing executive assisted by the I.T. department (Mail server information and the OI Platform will be required of them amongst other things).
- The TRANSFORM Workstream could be led by the production or operations executive.
- The SCALE workstream could be led by the HR executive.

These (potentially four) executives, inclusive of the Chief Executive, need to be provided with information with regard to their OI Work Stream roles. It is at this point that an OI Executive Workshop would be useful in terms of preparing the executives to lead their respective OI Work-Steams.

Once these executives are ready to build their stream, they will need to identify who is going to work with them on their respective OI Workstreams. The first person (after the respective OI Workstream lead) that is to be identified, per Stream, is the person who will be coaching the Workstream Lead and the workstream members in OI. This person will be responsible for making sure that OI discussions occur as planned, and that these discussions proceed in a way to be as value-adding as possible. This person will essentially assist the OI Work Stream Lead to manage the stream. The OI Streams described above are not constituted of full-time OI roles. They are part-time roles - people who meet weekly or ad-hoc, but only *after* feeding back progress details about their specific OI Stream Tasks with an e-mail or online report on their various activities for that week. It is important to not waste time providing feedback during these weekly discussions – these weekly discussions will be the place where real issues are discussed and actions or escalations are agreed. Meetings are intended to be for valuable collaboration - not simply feedback.

In this weekly meeting, important messages will be conveyed and top issues and high-level risks discussed. These meetings are not intended to be meetings for meeting sake, they are intended to be quick, highly effective and are the conduit for channeling risks and issues to senior management.

When the candidates for the respective OI Workstreams have been identified and the OI Lead Coach has been 'recruited' then the on-boarding event can take place. This is when all the people chosen to be in OI Workstreams are invited to an auditorium or any presentation area and, without causing 'death by power-point', educated in as creative and exciting a way as possible about the reasons for the OI with a focus on data that matters and how the OI Workstreams will work in order to achieve the desired-state of the organization. Put energy and enthusiasm into your communications – not just content.

At this point people may be asking, 'Why do we need to get ALL of these people involved?' You might relate the Aesop fable about the farmer and his sons in Chapter One. Good Change is like a fast-spreading fatal disease – the more people infected with the new way of doing business, the quicker the old way will die.

After the on-boarding event has taken place, the OI Workstreams need to be 'kicked-off' individually. Some people may be involved in more than one team, and that is acceptable, but try to get as many different people in the OI Workstreams as possible. The individual OI Workstream kick-off meetings will include the OI Lead Executive for the team, giving a leadership message in as far as the importance of the OI Workstream achieving its goals.

A presentation of how the respective team will operate in terms of process, actions, feedback loops and governance could be done. Please remember: the Aesop principle must be understood. *The key outcome of the team is to have involved as many other people in the various Change activities as possible, whilst achieving the Change Team objectives.*

Once the OI Workstream has been kicked-off with a healthy number of team-members, then organization is ready to be 'OI Active'!

Tips on selecting people for the OI Workstreams.

There will always be people who are negative towards the OI and seemingly always bad mouth people trying to do the OI. An effective OI Workstream is one with a balanced view of what needs to be done. The negative types - people who are committed to clients and the success of the organization - can sometimes be very valuable in balancing the activities and providing a critical view on things. Quite often, people who are perceived to be negative have been included in an OI Workstream and their value has been a more practical approach to a problem and they are quite good at identifying risks. So consider a balanced team, invite the positive go-getters and... also invite the cynics.

In small companies, you may only have three or four people per team, and even then they may be in the other teams too. In some instances, depending on the size of the organization, you may have forty people ***per*** OI Workstream. What is highly important is that as many people participate in OI activities as possible.

Often, OI Leads are not the delegating type and they attempt to do everything themselves. This is contrary to the real founding principle of Change Management, and that is to try and get as many people doing the Change as possible. Invite the coffee barista, invite the warehouse manager, you will be surprised at how many people will want to join the teams. These are not full-time teams, they meet weekly to discuss issues and collaborate to facilitate the OI process and will do OI activities depending on what OI Workstream they are in, but this effort needs to be done in consideration with their daily tasks. Whilst some companies are busier than others there is one thing to bear in mind, every hour of OI preparation invested before the new way of doing business is switched on, could be saving weeks of problem fixing, and loads of money wasted because of confusion and lack of understanding of the new way.

Tips on preparing executives for their Change Lead role.

Once the executives have signed the OI Workstream contracting document and are ready for their role as OI Lead for their respective stream, it is a good idea to use the Executive OI Lead training offered by an external OI Practice. Some people may work on more than one OI work-Stream. These streams need to be activated and in the Activate Sessions people will need to be educated about what it is they will be doing.

37

IMPLEMENTING OI WITH THE OI VALUE CHAIN

The following chapters will present nine activities divided equally into the three steps of the OI Value Chain, to implement OI in the organization and start doing OI. They are:

1. *DESIGN,*
2. *TRANSFORM,*
3. *SCALE.*

Hopefully this is becoming familiar to you by now! Introductions to OI Value Chain approaches and the nine steps to consider in implementing Organizational Innovation at an organization, are as follows:

1. OI DESIGN

The derivation of the strategic business case for being 'OI Active', worked-out with executives, is key in starting to implement OI Practices. This business case is what normally initiates implementing OI in an organization.

Here are some suggested steps:

1.1 **Executive Introduction,** using the CoachOI.com 'Onboarding Executives' Presentation an OI Practice Leader with familiarity of how to present this specific presentation, will seek to obtain executive approval to proceed with the following step.

1.2 **OI Business Case,** with approval as above, to interview key stakeholders and executives around OI subjects, the OI Practice Leader, either an external or internal person, will collect data about the need to introduce OI into the organization.

1.1 **OI Policy Executive Workshop,** assuming the business case is accepted, the OI Practice Lead, will assist the executives to align on the scope and resources that particular organization has agreed to commit to, for OI.

2. OI TRANSFORMATION

The following three implementation steps are required to TRANSFORM the organization to have the required resources and context in place for OI Capabilities to do their work. These are the things that will be used by the OI Innovators and Coaches to manage all OIs across the organization.

2.1 **OI Ignition** All the charters, governance and frameworks are explored, discussed, documented and agreed (signed-off). The focus is on familiarization by the OI Leads and OI Practice Lead in order to prepare for the development of OI Capabilities with all the respective OI Workstream charters (Available for download at CoachOI.com). These are then communicated to managers at all levels, with training being scheduled for them, to learn how to coach OI.

2.2 **Ownership** – Senior management, responsible for OI Workstreams, must agree in writing that they will do specific activities required of them as OI Leaders. We call these agreements this OI Contracting, a social contract with specific performance measures in terms of meeting attendance, budget etc. It is advised that they go through OI Executive Readiness Training.

2.3 **Build the Workstreams** – The people who have been invited into these workstreams will be working on one of the five OI principles (as per the previous chapters in this book):

      1. Coaching OI Workstream,
      2. Success Journeys Workstream,
      3. DESIGN Workstream,
      4. TRANSFORM Workstream,
      5. SCALE Workstream,

3. OI SCALE

The following three OI Activities will be the ***doing*** part of the OI Value Chain and are activated *per OI*. Adhering to the OI Platform processes ***will*** enable processes to design, transform, and scale in a way that is managed, inasmuch as OIs can be managed. They will also prepare the stakeholder groups in the SCALE step of the Value Chain.

2.1 **DESIGN** – Refer to the DESIGN Chapter

2.2 **TRANSFORM** – Refer to the TRANSFORM chapter

2.3 **SCALE** - Refer to the SCALE Chapter

As was mentioned, we're implementing OI just as we would do an OI in the organization. It's no different! An OI Implementation review will document to what degree the OI Objectives were met and the OI can be signed-off as, 'Active'.

The next chapters will explain the activities and examples of deliverables required within the 2. TRANSFORM and 3. SCALE steps. It's a more operational explanation of what was covered in the DESIGN, TRANSFORM and SCALE chapters.

38

OI TRANSFORMATION

Coaching OI Workstream.

An Organization-wide kick-off event will indicate to stakeholders, the seriousness of OI for the organization.. This event can ignite also, a recruitment drive to sign-up employees and other stakeholders to get involved with OI as OI Coaches or OI Innovators, or within the OI Workstreams.

More often than not, OI requires managing the people-side of change, and managing change is seen to be a process of 'soft', generally unknown activities. But the people-side of change must be led by the highest accessible executive. It is for this very reason that senior management must be physically signed into their OI roles, taking ownership of the OI is required to ensure its success. At the very beginning, it is necessary to get the executive mind-set OI-Centric and the role that they are to play, in order for OI to be successful.

As OI in enterprises brings about TRANSFORMATION which is generally associated with resistance (which is an intelligent response) the traditional executive may prefer to delegate managing change - typically to an HR executive or a psychologist fulfilling the consulting role of Change Management Lead.

However, managing and leading OI is so much more than just dealing with people's emotions and getting people excited through creative communication campaigns.

It is most important that executives understand their role in OI and all the OIs that may be in the OI Pipeline – and commit to it in writing, that *they* will *LEAD and SUPPORT* the OI no matter how scary it may seem, with advisory stakeholders who can support and in some cases do the work required, but never taking the lead, so to speak.

We refer to this as 'OI Lead Contracting'. It is a principle that is captured in a document outlining what each party expects from the other - between executives and the respective internal or external OI Practice.

Examples are:
- I will attend a minimum of 90% of the OI meetings to be held weekly.
- I will read all documentation respective to the OI within three working days.
- I will raise concerns about things before meetings take place in order to resolve them before meetings,

These agreements explicitly outline what is expected of the OI Lead and the OI Practice. They then need to *sign the OI Commitment document and commit in spirit, to OI.* (This is the singular most important part of OI and possibly the most testing for an executive.)

A useful preceding activity in preparation of the owner-contracting process is to arrange a meeting with the CEO or highest ranking accessible executive 'The OI Lead', to obtain,

- a verbal agreement that OI Ownership lies at the executive level.
- that the CEO (or highest ranking accessible executive) will take on the role of OI Lead.
- that the OI Lead will ask their subordinate or peer executives to take OI Lead roles of the various OI Workstreams.

After the OI Leadership contracting is done, which means that the Executive OI Leads have signed and committed to the OI Lead in the contracting document and, more importantly, the actual process of OI, then the OI Workstream Charter needs to be developed and signed-off, for each OI Workstream.

Stakeholder Analysis *needs* to be *done!!* Once the analysis is done, there won't be too many changes to the stakeholder group information - perhaps, only how many people in that group are going to be affected by the OI, per OI. Stakeholder data analysis is almost a once-off activity, but this analysis data must be maintained throughout the OI process if key details about stakeholders are changed.

Stakeholder management and engagement, at this point, is at the key-stakeholder level, merely introducing certain OI concepts to key individuals and beginning to obtain their support of the high-level view of the desired state.

If OIs have failed previously, it might be best to do a lot of education targeted at key-stakeholders helping them understand why a new OI will **NOT** fail.

In the OI TRANSFORM phase before starting to do OI, all of the datasets containing stakeholder details at an individual level will have been uploaded to the OI Platform.

Key stakeholders could at this point be educated about their role as key-stakeholder and for which stakeholder groups they are responsible. Further education about how the communications will be channelled could also be done, thus giving them a holistic view of the 'push', 'pull', 'profile' communications processes, as set out in the SCALE Workstream Charter and its framework.

Success Journey Workstream.

This stream will begin by building a stakeholder group

database in the OI Platform, as part of the OI Platform, begin configuring it as you require. Start by building the stakeholder group profiles. So, for example, based on the points in the chapter earlier in this book about stakeholder analysis, collect the information from the signed-off Stakeholder Analysis document. This would be, for example, the stakeholder group name such as 'External Customers' or the 'Central Distribution Warehouse Employees'.

Within this profile group OI Innovators will determine by way of an indicator field or column (if you are going to do this in a spreadsheet) whether the respective stakeholder group will be directly or indirectly be affected by their OI. This will assist the SCALE Workstream in identifying easily who needs what communications, accordingly. Alternatively, when conducting the Business Impact Analysis, you can study each changing business process or aspect of business that might be affected by the OI and identify which stakeholder groups will be impacted by changes in that specific process. This stakeholder impact analysis if linked back to the stakeholder record, to assess the impact on specific stakeholder groups will enable more effective and focused OI communications to that stakeholder group.

DESIGN Workstream.

This workstream focuses on developing design-thinking workshops around the organization, developing a design-thinking culture, related to OI. Please look at the d.school website for content.

TRANSFORM Workstream.

This particular aspect of OI does not feature as often as it could be in business projects, yet its objectives are key to successful, sustainable OIs. Business Impact Management is the alignment of organizational *aspects* to the new way of doing business.

The chapter referring to 'TRANSFORM', outlines what the objectives of this exercise are, per OI. However for the OI TRANSFORM phase of implementing OI, the Transformation Charter is the primary deliverable for this step. It will outline the process as set out in the respective chapter. What probably requires the most emphasis is how the process will be governed and how line-managers will be measured on their response to requirements for alignment workshops and departmental alignment sessions. This is where specific changes related to OI are going to affect how managers, manage for example, and the impact of these changes need to be clearly understood by the impacted managers, employees and other relevant stakeholders.

In the TRANSFORM part of implementing OI, only the approach (TRANSFORM Charter, signed-off) and education sessions about analyzing and mapping business impacts of implementing OI, need to be completed.

SCALE Workstream.

In OI TRANSFORM, the SCALE Team's activities in this step relates to obtaining the respective 'master data' that represents the learning landscape. The SCALE Workstreams will benefit from seeking to build a database (or use the OI Platform) of all things related to customers, employees, training material, courses, training venues, trainers etc. that will be part of the Scale Plan.

Start with a strategy workshop with stakeholders who are close to the project and get them to answer fundamental questions such as:

- Define the Scale Plans
- When should the communications start?
- When should the education start?
- When should the training start?
- What developmental or personal mastery objectives should be developed?
- By when must the training be complete?

- Should the training be split by identifying what is critical and required before the go-live day, and what is non-critical and can be trained after go-live day?
- Capacity planning: How many people are we enabling through education, training and other learning and developmental activities?
- Capacity planning: Based on the new processes and/or system learning requirements, how many education, training and developmental events are we expecting to do? More or less will do, at this point.
- How many rooms do we have that we can use for these events?
- How many people per venue?
- What are the learning instruments? Computers, Machinery etc.
- How many of these do we have available for training?
- Will we create centralized training centers or will we create training venues at the various sites?
- Do we train our people or should we outsource this requirement?
- Do we believe that we are really too busy to train during regular hours and will thus have to train after hours?
- Who will do the training documentation? Who will QA

the training documentation?
- What education items are likely to be required, new policies or processes? Etc.
- How is education and training going to be incorporated when new-employees start with the company, or existing employees are given new roles?
- How are diversity principles going to be implemented, thus improving an organization's diversity targets?

A mind-map of all the details that you believe will define the parameters in which the Communication, Education and Training processes must be executed, will be helpful. Once the mind-map is complete, develop the SCALE Charter document with the concepts derived from the mind-map points and structure. Include a developmental program for people who will be an important part of *supporting* others through the process of SCALing OIs. These people could be line-managers or non-management people who have been identified as being able and willing to assist others in times of need or give advice about particular aspects of business — especially related to the new way of doing business.

This process of developing key people, who will be first-line support, will logically assist the embedding of support processes. In I.T. projects they are often referred to as

Super-users, or Power-users. As discussed previously in the chapter on communications, *OI* communications requires two-way channels to always be in place, with profiling to understand where the risks are from a perception perspective:

- **'*PUSH*'** Communications: Executive messages, newsletters, e-mails, posters, conferences, workshops, road-shows etc.
- **'*PULL*'** Communications that can be accessed by stakeholders, like a FAQ Database or website.
- **'*PROFILE*'** Communications: Surveys, interviews, workshops etc. identifying the highest perception risks indicating where more communications may need to be focussed.

The framework for these communications can be included in the OI SCALE Plan.

'Push' Communications:

As communications involves public relations work, it is critical at this point that the interactions between stakeholders and the Change project are looked after very well. Anybody in a key role at this point who has negative or destructive feelings about the Change, will need special attention in terms of understanding their concerns -

indicating where in the Change Process those risks will be mitigated.

BTW, in practice, OI-Branding (giving your OI a name) is NOT advised, as this creates inter company competition for no real purpose. OI Numbering will work just fine to communicate about OIs, and also make sure that no OI is singularly different to the organization, all OIs should be seen as 'business as usual', like a purchase order number, the process is the same, but the content is different and identified by a number.

Lessons from marketing principles should be understood and applied, with particular respect to what a story is, and how to craft great stories which form the narrative around the OI, like 'Why are we doing this?' We also call this messaging.

Within the OI SCALE Workstream Charter, principles related to Public Relations, Marketing (Promoting, Publicity, Advertising) communication channels etc., can be highlighted and included in the OI SCALE Framework.

'Pull' Communications:

It's useful for stakeholders to be able to access information related to the OI from somewhere, insofar as it is allowed.

'Profile' Communications:

There are multiple 'Profile' methods the most popular being surveys and interviews . In 'fear' cultures, it is important to ensure that stakeholders being surveyed or interviewed are assured of anonymity.

Note: All communications requirements can be enabled by the OIActive.com *platform.*

39

OI SCALE

>>>Ultimately, every organization wants to be 'OI Active'.

Once OI TRANSFORMATION is done, then an organization can be said to be 'OI Active'. This means that the OI Executives are in place, OI Workstreams have been created and the OI Platform is prepared, then OI can really begin. It starts by SCALING UP OI into the organization, team by team.

Coaching OI Workstream.
Senior management involvement in OI as OI Leaders becomes very relevant at this point as key decision-making and influence with executive peers is required when it comes to cross-functional decision-making and addressing policy, procedure and system OIs. For the most part, activities within the OI Workstreams can continue without too much senior management involvement but those crucial areas

where they are required will make a difference between a successful or failed OI SCALing.

The great thing about having senior level involvement within the OI Workstreams is that the executives are kept up to date on planned new ways of doing business within the changing business environment and so, when making high-level decisions they will be more familiar with the context of the Change framework and have first-hand knowledge of potential impacts.

Another good reason for having senior management lead the teams is that they will be able to prioritize Change Activities within the ranks.

All the OI Workstreams have objectives that need to be reached and whilst self-governance is always the objective, there may be issues blocking progress on these activities, for example, perhaps the main reception area has been identified as a Change communications venue but authorization to do so has been elusive, this is where the OI Workstream Lead executive can take things in hand and arrange authorizations. There will be many instances where their executive influence will help things along.

The help goes both ways as, when the organization switches on the new way of doing business, that executive will be on par with how their business area is meant to operate and can make further educated decisions when things are going somewhat unexpectedly, the result of which could impair customer service or create other business concerns.

When executives are seen to be involved in 'doing' the Change, stakeholders and shareholders will appreciate the importance of the Change. Also, their perception of the executive body may improve adding credibility to the organization.

More and more frequently, according to an executive headhunter, clients are asking for executives that have led complex corporate-wide Change, as effective Change is becoming increasingly important to organizations, not only in South Africa.

Success Journey Workstream.

Managing the expectations of stakeholders is critical in terms of avoiding disappointment. This is why it is a fundamental point, to have selected key stakeholders who are already integrated into stakeholder groups like suppliers, and manage the expectations of their respective groups. Whilst stakeholder management is important in providing a stakeholder radar and keeping a database of contact details for communication purposes, the people involved here are key in identifying and mitigating stakeholder risk.

This risk can be from unions, customers, even government, wherever a stakeholder group can influence the outcome of the project or the stability of post-go-live operations, there must be an influential key stakeholder on the Success Journey Workstream to bring these risks and issues to the table so that mitigating actions can be put in place.

DESIGN Workstream.

This workstream focuses on developing design-thinking workshops around the organization, developing a design-thinking culture, related to OI. Please look at the d.school website for content.

TRANSFORM Workstream.

This is an area of Change that is so critical but very seldom done adequately. A reason for this could be, because many people, *even* people calling themselves Change Management Specialists know very little about it. This is mostly because the Change Management Industry is filled with psychologists and communications people with very little business analysis experience and system architecture knowledge. Only seasoned psychologists, or psychologists who have been a part of business processes in operations for example, will have a real knowledge of process and system integration.

The TRANSFORM Workstream has everything to do with understanding processes, policy structures, systems, strategic performance structures and how the desired business state is going to affect these business aspects in its current state.

The TRANSFORM Workstream, that will manage the business impacts and get business aligned to the new way, can begin collecting basic information such as:

- What functional areas of business are being impacted e.g.: Finance, HR and Warehousing.
- Once this has been confirmed, then the identification of the roles, policies, processes, strategic KPIs, systems and standard operating procedures being impacted within these functions needs to take place e.g.: Controlling Accounts, Accounts Payable, Accounts Receivable, Cash Management, Asset Management.
- Once these key processes have been listed, then roles within these processes need to be identified and mapped to the processes e.g.: Accounts Receivable Clerk mapped to Accounts Receivable process.

The next step is to invite the business and system analysts (sometimes the same person) to identify impacts on these processes and roles, then have them describe the complexity and importance of getting the people aligned in time e.g.: A new chart of accounts listed under the process 'Controlling Accounts'.

Once all the foreseeable impacts have been identified and registered (preferably using the OI Platform), then the invitation to view impacts and register more impacts can go out to other stakeholders. This is so that, they too can have a chance to register impacts as and when they learn more about the desired state of the organization.

Once the known impacts have been registered, (for the average medium-sized organization going through company-wide OI, it could be in the 'hundreds'), then the process of assigning ownership of alignment activities begins. Those people on the Transformation Workstream can be assigned ownership of individual impacts. It does not necessarily mean that they will be doing all the alignment work, but rather that they will inspire their peers to do some of the alignment activities, such as talking to warehouse staff about new shelving lay-outs in the warehouse.

Once ownership has been accepted for an impact, the process of developing alignment plans - begins. Take the example of the Change in the organization's financial chart of

accounts. An alignment activities plan could have the following alignment activities:
- Communicate in a meeting with head-office finance staff,
- Head-office staff to communicate with their respective finance people at other production facilities or branches - this is known cascading communication.

The OI which is being taken through the OI Value Chain will have dates against these deliverables, and deliverable owners are to be encouraged to keep the progress of their deliverables updated. This goes for all OI Workstream members.

As these alignment activities are being completed, there will be more impacts being registered that must also be assigned and the respective stakeholders aligned.

Where there are issues, they will more than likely be because of new process policies conflicting with old business policies. These issues need to be escalated to the Business Impact Management Change Team Executive who will be able to influence policy makers into resolving the situation.

Scale Workstream.

Often confused with ***just*** training, 'enabling' is the full process of taking a person from operating effectively in one business state to operating just as effectively (***if not more***) in the new business state. In order to effectively enable a person, there must education, training, performance management and accountability processes in place. It is worth pausing a moment to consider those twelve years of school and further years of tertiary study, what school and tertiary education systems are supposed to do is **enable** those who are willing to become value-adding members of society through the application of intelligent thought evolving mankind. However, plainly, there is a severe lack of this enablement in most countries around the world. Similarly in organizations, this happens too. People are not enabled sufficiently enough in organizations to become value-adding members of the organizational community.

The main reason for this is possibly that the intent with regard to enabling is wrong. Where employees are not enabled adequately, it's quite possible that their employer/manager don't lead people effectively, and by this it is meant that they don't lead with care, neither do they lead with sincere intent to grow their people.

We care for our children adequately enough to hold them accountable for not cleaning their rooms, for example, deducting pocket money or putting a ban on gaming until the lesson is learnt. However, in the work place, it seems we don't care enough to hold people accountable.

It is common that, to be held accountable in the workplace there is a negative connotation, largely because, where it has been done, it has been done incorrectly.

Holding people accountable is a leadership process that few understand. Too often, people are scolded in front of their peers, for example. These approaches do not lead to constructive empowerment processes. A true leader will hold the person accountable with the intent that the person becomes aware of their error and through a constructive feedback loop will lead them increasing their capability.

Sincere and genuine enabling comes down to intent, always treat the people who need to be enabled with care and become integrated into their aspirations for growth. Help them achieve their personal desired state, and they will internalize the Change objectives as it serves the community, making their career objectives more realistic and sustainable.

Once the direction of the SCALE Team has been agreed and is clear to stakeholders, the practical work of identifying who needs what communication, education or training, and how to deliver this service, begins.

Working from the TRANSFORM Charter and subsequent SCALE Plan model, preparation of education session material, OI Platform training material, role definitions, job description updates etc., all take place. It is important that unions get a view of the HR implications and in order to foster a good relationship with employees and unions, invite them to these role definition workshops which is the basis for empowerment, and give the people a sense of comfort that no discussions are being held behind closed doors. Any additional work/job enlargement must be treated as an HR item for discussion through the proper consultative processes with impacted employees.

As the process of 'who must be given what communication, education and training' continues, so preparations for delivering education sessions and training classes begins. It is really important to have all this planned far in advance so as to give the respective line-managers sufficient notice, in order for them to manage the people to be on whichever courses they need to be on without, for example, disrupting customer service.

Coaching OI can be hugely rewarding for the right profile of manager. Encouraging subordinates to grow through attending sessions, will also increase the leadership legitimacy of the manager, with the spin-off that their people are actually being prepared for the new way of doing business by understanding what is expected of them in the newly formulated roles.

In implementing OI in the an organization, the more that these principles that are upheld in the proper spirit, the better the outcome will be – so do it right, with the right intent and investment.

'PUSH & PULL' Communications.

These could be OI posters advertising reasons for an implementing OI, or road-shows introducing a OI. The approach that was developed as part of the SCALE Plan for the respective charter in the DESIGN phase should NOT be affected by the results of the survey because the framework should have planned 'push'/'pull'/'profile' communications cycles, molding and shifting mind-sets in a way that is aligned to what is needed, OI. This means that all communications will and/or have been adequately planned and executed. Keep knee-jerk communications and shooting from the hip communications minimal. Plan the work, work the plan.

The 'profiling' feedback will influence the content of the 'push' and 'pull' communication channels.

Make sure that your key 'push/pull' communications does the job of mitigating the identified risks. The next round of communication activities can reflect the effects of the 'profiling' communications activities by way of the top risks in the previous survey being shifted down the list of risks and having possibly become enablers of the OI. So the fear of job-loss can be changed to relief, certainly many people will now be positive and supportive of the OI as they begin to understand the Change Project objectives more.

Communications Profiling

The first 'pull' communications about the organization implementing OI, in the OI TRANSFORM step, part of the OI Implementation, is to go through a feedback loop communications process. By this we mean, listen to what the people are saying about OI, using surveys, interviews and discussion groups. If you choose to use the OI Platform, then the process is quite easy. The OI Platform contains all the online surveys and analysis engines for this requirement. The first thing that must be done is to ensure that all the e-mail addresses of the intended survey population are in the stakeholder database, or have been uploaded into the OI Platform. Once you can be sure that you have these details, then the process of building your survey instrument can begin. For starters you might consider some of the factors that are key to maintaining the micro-economic environment, such as impact on employees, customers and the organization's operational stability. Once you have identified the important impact areas of your organization, a set of survey and one-on-one interview questions can be built that can gauge the strength of negative or positive perceptions of, for example: the degree to which line-managers are supporting their departments in adopting OI approaches.

Once a communication has been sent out requesting people to complete the survey, (the link of which can be placed on the project website or in the e-mail) make sure you have asked them to have it completed before a certain point in time. The SCALE Workstream Executive Lead can ask the OI SCALE Workstream member to work with the respective Key Stakeholder, to mail out a request asking affected employees to participate. The percentage of people participating varies widely. 100% response rates have been experienced in some organizations, down to 30% and less response rates in others. Mostly there is hard work required to get a high response rate on the survey.

You could think of doing a competition in conjunction with the survey. Send out a survey 'cut-off extension' e-mail. Do whatever you can to get a high rate of survey responses, but do NOT FORCE a respondent to do so. In most cases these surveys are conducted on the principle of anonymity for the sake of attempting to obtain a higher level of honesty and therefore a more reliable risk profile. (Please remember that this entire process can be done online using the OI Platform)

This first survey provides a baseline profile and will most likely reflect weak to negative responses about implementing OI, depending on what has been communicated formally and informally, and based on the perceives success, of the OI population, people who are targeted to be directly involved with OI in the the organization. This is because most people will not know anything about OI at this point in the project and only a handful of people with intimate knowledge of the OI will have any support for OI. It is basically a set of results that reflects the true nature of the situation and that is, OI hasn't started yet.

Two or maybe three more 'pull' activities can happen. If the principles of OI as described in this book are followed, the numbers will reflect an improvement in the Change readiness of the organization. The graphs may indicate an improvement over the time that the 'pull' activities take place, which will be set at intervals throughout the OI SCALE Process - including one a little while after the OI SCALE Plans are completed and the organization is fully OI Active.

In compiling a report based on the survey feedback, provide a consultative explanation on the results. Certain trends or statistical results may reflect a theory prevalent amongst management as to why for example, a certain group of employees who have been in the organization for between eight and eleven years seem to be especially averse to OI. If you look at the company's history, you may find that between eight and eleven years ago a corporate-wide OI was initiated that brought about downsizing and this has brought back very unhappy memories of colleagues losing their jobs and they themselves having lived with uncertainty because of some new OI.

On the quantitative reporting of these surveys, the results are to be sorted so as to reflect the most negatively answered questions on the top of the list. For example if the survey was compiled of 30 questions, they could be listed together by sorting the questions, from the question with the most overall negative result, down to the most positive. If you take the top five questions, these are the ones that your surveyed population have the biggest concerns about. This list becomes your risk profile for which you might use specially crafted communications to mitigate the negativity of the population's perceptions – whilst actually doing something about their concerns. For example, if the top most negative risk is with regard to people fearing for their jobs, then 'push' communications that are widespread and assure that OI is not meant to reduce headcount, but rather to introduce a new way of doing business. *(Note: If the Change objective is to downsize an organization, then you I advise to read books relating to downsizing specifically, which is a different subject altogether. Although the principles in this book could help in this kind of OI, special attention must be given to how those employees identified for retrenchment need to be cared for in terms of providing them with market-skills.)*

40

OI ACTIVE!

Once OI is Active, its really time to celebrate! A final sign-off session which considers the implementation vision of OI, can be held in which all of the related signees of the commitment to implement OI, unanimously agree that OI has been implemented.

Don't forget to thank the people who together broke their own stick to make it happen (Aesop).

When the organization starts activating departmental OIs, do the same thing, encourage them to celebrate, and thank the people who made it happen, hopefully it'll include a financial payout too, relative to the added the value of the OI, to the OI Innovator.

41

YOUR OWN OI PRACTICE

If you've been through the four sections of this book and have a grasp on the potential value of OI, then you might begin thinking of your future and how to use OI. You could use it in either your department, as a manager coaching OI, or as a trusted adviser to organizations, private, listed, government or non-profit. Either way, registering an OI Practice on *CoachOI.com* is the starting point, as that's where access to the *OIActive.com* setup requests and all the related templates and artifacts can be accessed. Anyone can login at *CoachOI.com* and request to have OI Active setup for their enterprise. At *CoachOI.com*, you have access to content, learning material and direct access to the OI Global Mentor group who can assist you in doing OI in your department or organization, or growing your OI Practice.

As an external trusted adviser you may want to introduce OI to your clients. Once you create your OI Practice page at *CoachOI.com* then you can create client-team membership and help client managers to become OI Coaches.

Have a look for the OI Practice Playbook at *CoachOI.com*. The kind of work an OI Practice owner will do, is develop managers into OI Coaches, starting with 'Coaching OI Professional Certification', a three day workshop. In this workshop, delegates will work through this book, with extra content, videos, facilitated learning processes and group exercises. This will assist delegates to have a deeper understanding of the four sections of this book, being:

1. Introduction to OI
2. Success Journeys and OI Value Chain
3. Coach OI
4. Implement OI

Internal Project Managers, Change Managers and Internal Consultants have the right backgrounds to easily grasp the vision of OI, and thus can easily develop an OI Practice in house, working with managers across the organization to become OI Coaches for their department.

To setup a registered OI Practice, receive an OI Practice Registration Number, with access to licensed material, please signup at *CoachOI.com* and access the guided process to do this, online. Whilst the phrase is new, and the semantics are simplified, they approaches will be familiar to anyone with experience in managing projects and transformations. As part of developing your OI Practice as a private external adviser, or internal to serve the needs of an organization, or the head of a large department who wants an OI Practice to focus on developing that departments managers into OI Coaches, the roadmap to be successful is the same. However, additional support is provided to OI Practice owners who are private advisers and need assistance with marketing, and selling their OI Services to client organizations. If you are a global organization and require support in to create many practices around the world, in many different countries, that's supported on *CoachOI.com* too. To clarify your intention, select the correct practice type when you create your practice on *CoachOI.com* by selecting one of the following options:

1. Global OI Practice
2. Advisory OI Practice
3. VP OI Practice
4. Departmental OI Practice
5. Manager OI Practice

(Others may be added for convenience.)

For each type, there is a roadmap with OI Platform links and training videos to assist you to get your OI Practice. As a registered practice owner, you will receive special invitations to webinars and Global Mentor meetings discussing hot topics and OI Platform updates.

42

THE COACH OI GLOBAL LEADERSHIP TEAM

Exceptional OI Practice Owners will be invited to join the Coach OI Global Leadership Team (GLT) who partake in the direction-setting of Coach OI, globally and assist others to build their OI Practice and OI Skills.

Revenue-sharing is a functional motivation for these leaders to be as proactive as possible in targeting specific individuals, who may request individual mentors to partner with them, on the OI Practice journey.

43

COACHING OI AS A STARTUP

Coaching OI is a very new topic, built on the 'shoulders of giants' like Project Management (PMI) and Change Management (PROSCI). We ask that you're patient with us as we are a relatively new startup in the knowledge sense, and will greatly appreciate your support and understanding whilst we get somethings right on the platform and in content, like this book. As they say in Silicon Valley, if you're not embarrassed by your new product, then it's too late. We are always happy to talk with people interested in OI, OI Coaches and OI Practice Owners, just access the chat window at CoachOI.com. Let us know about any related issues or questions.

If you're happy with this 'startup' status we are in, then we look forward to learning and growing together along this journey, as the potential of this subject unfolds for everyone.

44

COACHING OI AS A SERVICE

Coaching OI as a service, can also be delivered online through video meetings to executives, managers, or OI Practice Owners who may want some guidance in the early days of their OI Journey.

There are also OI Global Mentors who can be accessed for assistance with implementing OI at organizations at a global, regional, national or local level.

To find out more, please look on *CoachOI.com* for more information on how the Coach OI team can partner with your OI Journey, and get learning live, from an OI Global Mentor.

ABOUT THE AUTHOR

Paul has nearly 30 years experience in leading transformation projects, the last 20 using SAP to build integrated cross-functional capabilities. Now with SAP S/4 HANA, he helps clients achieve their strategic objectives implementing short, medium and long term technology solutions that help to solve the right problems.

After working with Stanford University building an OI digital platform for the School of Medicine 3DQLab, he put design-thinking at the forefront of his projects. The Stanford School of Design taught him about using empathy to really help understand how to build solutions that solve real problems. Now he uses Organizational Innovation to implement SAP S/4HANA, Fiori, SAP Apps, Leonardo and all the latest SAP Tech, to help solve his client's most complex challenges.

From his early years transforming a Supply Chain and automating production in a factory he managed, overhauling a large retail culture, to building automotive databases for Toyota, he has always loved the nexus of people, technology and process, because that's all about creating Organizational Innovation.

He also runs the global Coach OI network, working with Global OI Leaders from around the world.

Website: *CoachOI.com*
Email: *paul.Wilson@CoachOI.com*

Printed in Poland
by Amazon Fulfillment
Poland Sp. z o.o., Wrocław